A SHAMBHALA THRESHOLD BOOK

THIS LONGING

Poetry, Teaching Stories, and Letters of Rumi

Jelaluddin Rumi

Versions by Coleman Barks and John Moyne

SHAMBHALA

Boulder

2000

SHAMBHALA PUBLICATIONS, INC.
2129 13th Street
Boulder, Colorado 80302
www.shambhala.com

Printed in the United States of America

Shambhala Publications makes every effort to print on acid–free,
recycled paper.

Shambhala Publications is distributed worldwide by Penguin
Random House, Inc., and its subsidiaries.

Library of Congress Cataloging-in-Publication Data
Jalal al-Din Rumi, Maulana, 1207–1273.
　　[Selections. English. 2000]
　　This longing: poetry, teaching stories, and letters of Rumi / translated by
Coleman Barks and John Moyne.
　　　　　　p. cm.
Includes bibliographical references.
ISBN 978-1-57062-533-6 (pbk.)
1. Sufi poetry, Persian—Translations into English. 2. Jalál al–Dån Råmå,
Maulana, 1207–1273—Correspondence. I. Barks, Coleman.
II. Moyne, John. III. Title.
PK6480. E5 B374　2000
891'.5511—dc21　　　　　　　　　　　　　　99–058184

BVG 01

CONTENTS

*This book is for Herb Barks, my brother,
and for Elizabeth Cox, Betsy, my sister.*

—C.B.

The Ocean of the Mathnawi

The *Mathnawi* is Rumi's masterwork, and it is impossible to give much sense of it in a selection of excerpts. It runs to six volumes, over fifty-one thousand verses of poetry, couplets in twelve-beat lines, in which the hemistichs, or half-lines, also rhyme. I have not tried, of course, to duplicate the music of the Persian. These versions of the *Mathnawi* are set in the free verse of American poetry, one of the strongest and most spiritually open and questing traditions in Western writing. But the majestic intricacy of the original, its reef-like porousness, cannot be brought over in free verse. The *Mathnawi* is complex, mature work, like Shakespeare's tragedies and the late romances, which cannot, of course, be translated, and yet they must.

To use Rumi's own metaphor, the *Mathnawi* is an ocean, with myriad elements swimming and adrift and growing in it: folklore, the *Qur'an*, stories of saints and teachers, myth, the sayings of Muhammed, jokes from the street, actual interruptions, whispered asides to Husam. There is an enormous generosity and humor at play here, and at work. Fresh, wild moments within a profound peace. Drunken, lyric dissolvings within a starry clarity. Spontaneous pleasure within discipline.

You may have heard the Sufi story about an Ocean-Frog who comes to visit a pond-frog, whose pond is three feet by four feet by two feet deep. The pond-frog is very eager and proud to show off the dimensions of his habitat, which in the story signify the limits of mind and desire. He dives down two feet to the bottom and comes up and asks, "Did you ever see water this deep? What is it like where you live?" The Ocean-Frog (from the Ocean of Ilm, the Divine Wisdom, which has no boundaries) cannot explain to the pond-frog what his Ocean home is *like*, but he says, "One day I'll take you there, and you can swim in it."

I am very much the pond-frog before the *Mathnawi*. I love the feel of its motions, its shifting variety, its music and its wisdom. The *Mathnawi* is a sacred text that invites one to drown in it. I don't claim to have done that. It's a continuing work, for me, this digging in Rumi's *Mathnawi*, to let the Ocean come up through the effort-places, to let the words drift away and the experience flood in (p. 63).

It's one of the most compelling texts, sacred or secular, that I know of. All I can do, really, is point to it, like some unlikely visitor from Chattanooga faced with the Himalayas.

* * *

The *Mathnawi* was spoken aloud and taken down by Rumi's beloved scribe, Husam Chelebi. The following story is told of how it began: The two were walking in the Meram vineyards outside Konya when Husam suggested that Mevlana begin a new work in a new form, something different from the odes and the quatrains, something in the *mathnawi* (couplets) tradition of Attar and Sanai and others. Rumi took a piece of paper from his turban and told Husam to read aloud what was on it. It was the opening of the *Mathnawi*, which Rumi had composed just that morning, the famous couplets spoken by the reed flute.

"There must be more," said Husam.
"If you will write for me, I will continue," replied Rumi.
"From this moment, I am your servant."

Thus the long, twelve-year process began. Husam describes it.

"He never took a pen in his hand while composing the *Mathnawi*. He would recite wherever he was, in the medrese (the dervish college), at the Ilgin hot springs, in the Konya baths, in the vineyards. When he started, I would write, and I often found it hard to keep up. Sometimes he would recite night and day for several days. Other times, he would compose nothing for months. Once for a period of two years he spoke no poetry. As each volume was completed, I would read it back to him, so that he could revise it."

The form, then, is an inspired and intuitively moving tapestry that can include anything it meets. A question from Husam, Arabic poetry, a surprise visitor, Quranic commentary, all get woven into One Vision, the pattern of which seems almost beyond human comprehension, as with the wonderful pun that Rumi uses to describe the daily motion of the sun as a weaver's shuttle (*maku*). *Ma ku*, in Persian, also means "Where are we?" so the weaving being done by the sun-shuttle back and forth, east to west, is also the repeated question, *Where are We?* with the implied pattern, and answer, not in sight. Not to the shuttle, anyway. (See pp. 37-8.) Likewise, the *Mathnawi's* whole truth may not be accessible to a particular reader standing in its surf, but the beauty and mystery of its Presence can be sensed.

* * *

Several of these *Mathnawi* segments are about teachers. It's a powerful theme throughout the six books, this longing for the Teacher, and for What Comes Through the Teacher.

> When matter dissolves in the Ocean
> the particles glow. As who I am now
> melts in a candleflame, identity
> becomes one vast motion.

> (#2)

Many images of expanded, particular identity come through: the adoration of Sunqur (p. 34), the melting of the Debtor Sheikh (p. 6), Noah in "As the Orchard is With the Rain" (p. 50), the end of "You Are Not a Single You" (p. 49). The mystery of the Oceanic Teacher is that of the *Mathnawi* itself. The only real analogy that I know of for its form is the actual presence of a Sufi teacher. The movements, sometimes abrupt, from narrative to lyric, from melting ecstasies to stern, practical advice, are very much the weavings of a collaboration between a teacher and a community of students. The dialectic of subject and next-subject and return to former subjects, the waiting, wandering, and finding, these are the unfolding waves that flow between a teacher and lively students in the Sufi tradi-

tion. The sense of collaboration is strong in the *Mathnawi*, of a poly-
logue going on, a group-work, of many being helped along by this
camel that can carry hundreds of mice across the river at once (p.
32).

A student once asked one of these teachers about the inner nature
of poetry. Punning and gently mimicking the student's Southern
accent, the teacher found the answer within the question. "Po-tree,
bo Tree! Poetry must be like the bo tree! Do you know how it grows?
Up, up, and then the long branches bend and where they touch
ground they send out roots and a new system begins."

The bo tree was also the tree under which the Buddha's enlight-
enment came. One feels that complex grounding and then the
ascending impulse in the *Mathnawi*. It is a poem full of rooted
human pain and foibles, but they are always understood from
above by the playfulness and atmospheric love that holds them. All
the splintered stories live within a compassionate intelligence, a
Humor (that word! from the Latin *umor*, wetness, so close to
Dante's *Amor*, ecstatic Love). We need a new coinage for the
swirling improvisation of this poem, an *Amor-Umor*.

The *Mathnawi* is a compendium of many elements, but the
reader-swimmer feels a *Gaia*-mind regulating the saline percent-
ages, keeping in balance the whole organism as well as the parts.
The *Mathnawi* is a text formed within a community and is itself a
community, a collection of poetries living within the large poem,
which is Rumi's Presence.

* * *

This selection also features Rumi's attention to animals. Their
endearing, familiar doings, as well as their ferocities and compul-
sions. They stand in the niches, above the doors and downspouts,
of Rumi's cathedral. They're everywhere. A baby pigeon hesitating
all day on the edge of its nest. A dog sniffing food, looking around,
sniffing again, and then eating. Behaviors we recognize, domestic
as well as wild and improbable: a gazelle put in with a herd of
donkeys, a dugong at night bringing a glowing pearl up on shore
to graze by the light of it. The animals are, most often, in some
difficulty. They signify the animal-soul torn between freedom and

confinement, and they are always themselves, very froggy and cocky and ducky and doggy and dugongy, even as they serve as symbols for the *nafs*, the energies that move and blind and block us at various stages in our growth.

The animals reveal, again, Rumi's grounded compassion, how meshed with the texture of living he is, as the wonderful *Letters* at the end of this volume also show. His deep surrender is one with a sure grasp of the practical and the daily. The edge of the wheel that touches the ground here, presses firmly into it. I don't mean to imply that he observes behavior like an experimental biologist, but he does watch closely, and always on the verge of laughter — the dog and the rooster, the mouse and the frog, and even the dream-puppies that bark inside the womb (p. 41). What could they be barking about? To keep watch? To start game? Or do they want to be fed? The embryo pups have none of those reasons, so he concludes they're like people who talk about something before they have the actual experience, who make idle talk on spiritual matters. "Still blind, they act as though they see." Rumi is tough on hypocrisy, and very complex in his treatment of the *nafs*. Perhaps the best image of how the animal-soul energies should be controlled is that of Jesus on the spindly donkey (p. 65), Jesus being the clear, rational soul and the donkey the *nafs-ammara*, or animal-soul.

Consider the characteristics of the donkey: It's transportation for the poor. It can carry large loads up a narrow path. It has a modest, steadfast, calm nature. Of even energy, patient, surefooted, not easily spooked. Not noble, not splendid, not high-strung, not used for war, and generally unimpressed with human authority, the donkey is more known for what it is *not*, than for what it is. The thin donkey gives many clues for the uses of controlled energy.

> Don't feed both sides of yourself equally.
> The spirit and the body carry different loads
> and require different attentions.
> > Too often
> we put saddlebags on Jesus and let the donkey
> run loose in the pasture.
> > Don't make the body do

what the Spirit does best, and don't put a big load
on the Spirit that the body could carry easily.

(pp. 71-2)

The snake, or the dragon, is Rumi's symbol for the *nafs* when
they're frighteningly out of control. See "The Snake-Catcher and
the Frozen Snake" (p. 67) as well as the snake-swallowing episode
of "Jesus on the Lean Donkey" (p. 65).

Hazrat Inayat Khan, who brought Sufism to the West in this
century, has this to say abut Rumi and the animal-soul energy, or
as he calls it, the *false ego*.

Rumi says your worst enemy is hiding within yourself,
and that enemy is your *nafs* or false ego. It is very difficult
to explain the meaning of this "false ego." The best I can do
is to say that every inclination which springs from disre-
gard of love, harmony, and beauty and which is concerned
with oneself and unconcerned with all others is the false
ego.

This enemy, Rumi says, develops. The more it is fed, the
stronger it becomes to fight with you; and the stronger it
becomes, the more it dominates your better self. There
comes a day when man is the slave of this enemy which is
hidden within himself. The worst position is to have an
enemy which one does not know. It is better to have a
thousand known enemies before one than to have one
within one and not to know it.

There are many meanings ascribed to the custom of
sages in India to have snakes around their necks. One of
those meanings is: "I have got it. It is still living, but now
I know that it is there, and it is my ornament." What does
this enemy breathe? This enemy breathes "I." Its breath is
always calling out, "I, separate from you, separate from
others, separate from everybody. My interest is mine; it
has nothing to do with others. The interest of others is
others' interest; it is not mine. I am a separate being."

Remember that no man is without it. If man was without it, he would never have said "I," because it is this enemy within him which is saying "I." The day this enemy is found and erased, or shed and crucified, that day the real "I" is found. But this "I" is a different "I." This "I" means you and I and everybody; it is an all "I."

* * *

Another theme is that of the *urgency* needed to burst open into love, and service, into the Ocean-Presence of the Teacher. Like the Hasidic saying, "Bake your bread with burning tears," the knot of God's generosity does not loosen until the halvah boy's sharp cry (p. 7). As God tells Moses, "I want burning, burning . . . Those who pay attention to ways of behaving and speaking are one sort. Lovers who burn are another" (p. 20). That torn-open-ness is what the reed flute, in the *Mathnawi's* opening passage, wants of its audience. "The music of the reed is fire, not air, . . . such longing. If I were also touching the lips of someone who spoke my language, I would tell all that could be told."

Husam Chelebi was a student of Shams. With him, then, the collaboration, the Connection, revives, the lover-Beloved, friend-and-Friend synapse, that is the subject of the *Divan*. Rumi called that huge collection of odes and quatrains *The Works of Shams of Tabriz*. Perhaps in a more concealed way, the stories and teaching of the *Mathnawi* come from that intense Shams-sun energy too. *Shams* means "the sun." The continuous ignition of moment *by* moment feels like the blood of that love flowing through this masterpiece.

And what of all the wine-talk? Some are troubled by it. Fermentation is one of the oldest symbols for human transformation. When the juice of grapes, under certain conditions, is closed up and allowed to incubate for a time, the results are spectacular. That change can also occur in people, and the sharing of the crushed-open mystery and joy is the cup passed around, is the Tavern, is

Whoever saw such drunkards?
Barrels broken open, the ground and starry

ceiling soaked. And look,
this full glass in my hand!

(p. 33, *Unseen Rain*)

The grapeskin O of the ego crushes underfoot, and a pouring begins, that's like the freedom death allows. This is the rubble stage, when pronouns no longer apply. Two drunks meet, and there's no differentiating them. But Rumi is clear: Look for the jewels within, and beyond, this Wine-drenched state. There is a sobriety that contains all drunkenness.

Here's the new rule: Break the wineglass
and fall toward the Glassblower's breath.

(p. 45, *Open Secret*)

and

Do that work, and you'll begin to hear *inside*
the maundering drunktalk of drunkards,
the Presence of the Winemaker, the Host
who served this wine to us.

(p. 73)

Drunkenness is Rumi's metaphor for the excitements of existence, which keep changing.

We feel freed from one noose,
and we run out yelling, *Justice for everybody*!

We think we're pure rain.
We don't see the next danger, how the road
we're on is matted with the hair
and bones of those who've gone before.

There's another region of excitements altogether.

One drop of that Wine,

and you'd never go back to these wines.

That's why God gave them,
so you can imagine the other.

(Mathnawi, III, 806ff)

* * *

One of the longings that I feel when I read the *Mathnawi* is for
community. The poetry and the teachings imply the joyful, and
strenuous, ebb and flow of a powerful matrix.

For a dervish, there must be a purpose,
a cause for existence, and inside the cause,
a True Human Being.

Learning communities are being built everywhere.
The whole world is a learning community!
Where is the True Human Being?

(#687)

Perhaps when longing takes such a fully expressive form as the
Mathnawi, the question becomes an answer. Jelaluddin Rumi is one
of the True Human Beings.

A metaphor for the dynamic between such a Guide, the human
mind, and the *nafs* is found in Book I, 2492ff, with the image of the
camel, the camel-driver, and the Sun (animal-soul, rational intel-
lect, Teacher).

The Holy Ones have an amber
that when they show it to you,
you want it more than anything.

When they conceal it, your surrendered love
becomes meanness and arrogance. You are to them
as animals are to human beings.

You're *subject* to saints, the Teachers,

the True Human Beings. Muhammed addressed
the whole world as, *My Servants* . . . .

Your intelligence is a camel-driver. You are the camel.
The Holy Ones are an Intelligence within your intellect.
Give your profoundest contemplation to this:

Camel, camel-driver, the Sun. There's only One Guide
for these hundreds of thousands of people, all
leading their camels. Develop an eye

that can see into the Sun. The world is nailed shut
in night, waiting for the Sun to come up.
And here it is, hidden in a speck of dirt!

Like a lion somehow disguised
in a fleece! Like an Ocean
beneath a piece of straw!

Coleman Barks

References

Nicholson, R. A. (1925-40). *The* Mathnawi *of Jalaluddin Rumi*. 8 vols. London:
Luzac & Co. Critical edition, translation, and commentary.

Selections from the Mathnawi

The Sheikh Who Played with Children

A certain young man was asking around,
"I need to find a wise person. I have a problem."

A bystander said, "There's no one with intelligence
in our town except that man over there
playing with the children,
                         the one riding the stick-horse.

He has keen, fiery insight and vast dignity
like the night-sky, but he conceals it
in the madness of child's play."

The young seeker approached the children, "Dear father,
you who have become as a child, tell me a secret."

"Go away. This is not a day
for secrets."
                    "But please! Ride your horse this way,
just for a minute."
                    The Sheikh play-galloped over.
"Speak quickly. I can't hold this one still for long.
Whoops. Don't let him kick you.
                        This is a wild one!"

The young man felt he couldn't ask his serious question
in the crazy atmosphere, so he joked,
                        "I need to get married.
Is there someone suitable on this street?"

"There are three kinds of women in the world.
Two are griefs, and one is a treasure to the Soul.
The first, when you marry her, is all yours.
The second is half-yours, and the third
is not yours at all.
                    Now get out of here,

before this horse kicks you in the head! Easy, now!"

The Sheikh rode off among the children.
The young man shouted, "Tell me more about the kinds of women!"

The Sheikh, on his cane horsie, came closer,
"The virgin of your first love is *all* yours.
She will make you feel happy and free. A childless widow
is the second. She will be half-yours. The third,
who is nothing to you, is a married woman with a child.
By her first husband she had a child, and all her love
goes into that child. She will have no connection with you.
Now watch out.
                          Back away.
                                          I'm going to turn this rascal around!"

He gave a loud whoop and rode back,
calling the children around him.

"One more question, Master!"
                                        The Sheikh circled,
"What is it? Quickly! That rider over there needs me.
I think I'm in love."
                          "What is this playing that you do?
Why do you hide your intelligence so?"
                                                  "The people here
want to put me in charge. They want me to be
Judge, Magistrate, and Interpreter of all the texts.

The Knowing I have doesn't want that. It wants to enjoy itself.
I am a plantation of sugarcane, and at the same time
I'm eating the sweetness."
                                  Knowledge that is acquired
is not like this. Those who have it worry if
audiences like it or not.
                          It's a bait for popularity.

4

Disputational knowing wants customers.
It has no soul.
                    Robust and energetic
before a responsive crowd, it slumps when no one is there.
The only real customer is God.
                              Chew quietly
your sweet sugarcane God-Love, and stay
playfully childish.
                    Your face
will turn rosy with illumination
like the redbud flowers.

(*Mathnawi*, II, 2338-2342, 2384-2385, 2400-2430, 2436-2438, 2442)

The Debtor Sheikh

Sheikh Ahmad was continually in debt.
He borrowed great sums from the wealthy
and gave it out to the poor dervishes of the world.
He built a Sufi monastery by borrowing,
and God was always paying his debts, turning sand
into flour for this Generous Friend.

The Prophet said that there were always two angels
praying in the market. One said, "Lord,
give the poor wanderer help." The other, "Lord,
give the miser a poison." Especially loud
is the former prayer when the wanderer is a prodigal
like Sheikh Ahmad, the Debtor Sheikh.

For years, until his death, he scattered seed profusely.
Even very near his death, with the signs of death clear,
he sat surrounded by creditors. The creditors in a circle,
and the great Sheikh in the center gently melting
into himself like a candle.

The creditors were so sour-faced with worry
that they could hardly breathe.

"Look at these despairing men," thought the Sheikh.
"Do they think God does not have four hundred gold dinars?"
Just at that moment a boy outside called,
                                    "Halvah, a sixth
of a dirhem for a piece! Fresh halvah!"
                                    Sheikh Ahmad,
with a nod of his head, directed the famulus
to go and buy the whole tray of halvah.

"Maybe if these creditors eat a little sweetness,
they won't look so bitterly on me."

The servant went to the boy, "How much for the whole lump
of halvah?"
"Half a dinar, and some change."

"Don't ask too much from Sufis, my son.
Half a dinar is enough."

The boy handed over the tray, and the servant brought it
to the Sheikh, who passed it among his creditor-guests.
"Please, eat, and be happy."

The tray was quickly emptied, and the boy asked the Sheikh
for his half a gold dinar.

"Where would I find such money? These men can tell you
how in debt I am, and besides, I am fast on my way
into non-existence."
The boy threw the tray on the floor
and started weeping loud and yelling,
"I wish
I had broken my legs before I came in here!
I wish
I'd stayed in the bathhouse today. You gluttonous,
plate-licking Sufis, washing your faces like cats!"

A crowd gathered. The boy continued, "O Sheikh,
my master will beat me if I come back without *any*thing."

The creditors joined in, "How could you do this?
You've devoured our properties, and now you add this
one last debt before you die.
Why?"

The Sheikh closes his eyes and does not answer.
The boy weeps until afternoon prayers. The Sheikh
withdraws underneath his coverlet,
pleased with everything,

pleased with Eternity, pleased with death,
and totally
unconcerned with all the reviling talk around him.

On a bright-moon night, do you think the moon,
cruising through the tenth house, can hear the dogs barking
down here?
But the dogs are doing what they're supposed to do.
Water does not lose its purity because of a bit of weed
floating in it.
That King drinks wine on the riverbank
until dawn, listening to the watermusic, not hearing
the frog-talk.
The money due the boy would have been
just a few pennies from each of his creditors, but the Sheikh's
spiritual power prevents that from happening.
No one gives the boy anything.

At afternoon prayers a servant comes with a tray
from Hatim, a friend of Ahmad's, and a man
of great property. A covered tray.

The Sheikh uncovers the face of the tray, and on it
there are four hundred gold dinars, and in one corner,
another half a dinar wrapped in a piece of paper.

Immediately the cries of abasement, "O King of Sheikhs,
Lord of the Lords of Mystery! Forgive us.
We were bumbling and crazed. We were knocking lamps over.
We were . . ."
"It's all right. You will not be held
responsible for what you've said or done. The secret here
is that I asked God and the way was shown

that until the boy's weeping, God's merciful generosity

8

was not loosened.

                    Let the boy be like the pupil of your eye.
If you want to wear a robe of spiritual sovereignty,
let your eyes weep with the wanting."

(Mathnawi, II, 376-444)

A Mouse and a Frog

A mouse and a frog meet every morning on the riverbank.
They sit in a nook of the ground and talk.

Each morning, the second they see each other,
they open easily, telling stories and dreams and secrets,
empty of any fear or suspicious holding-back.

To watch and listen to those two
is to understand how, as it's written,
sometimes when two beings come together,
Christ becomes visible.

The mouse starts laughing out a story he hasn't thought of
in five years, and the telling might take five years!
There's no blocking the speechflow-river-running-
all-carrying momentum
that true intimacy is.

Bitterness doesn't have a chance
with those two.

The God-Messenger, Khidr, touches a roasted fish.
It leaps off the grill
back into the water.

Friend sits by Friend, and the tablets appear.
They read the mysteries
off each other's foreheads.

But one day the mouse complains, "There are times
when I want *sohbet*,* and you're out in the water,
jumping around where you can't hear me.

*Spiritual conversation

We meet at this appointed time,
but the text says, *Lovers pray constantly.*

Once a day, once a week, five times an hour,
is not enough. Fish like we are
need the ocean around us!"

Do camel-bells say, *Let's meet back here Thursday night?*
Ridiculous. They jingle
together continuously,
talking while the camel walks.

Do you pay regular visits to *yourself*?
Don't argue or answer rationally.

Let us die,
                and dying, reply.

(*Mathnawi*, VI, 2632, 2665-2669, 2681-2684)

The Long String

The Mouse asks the Beloved Frog,
                              Do you know
what you are to me? During the day,
you're my energy for working. At night,
you're my deepest sleep.
                              But could we be together
outside of Time as well as inside?

Physically, we meet only at breakfast.
Your absence during the rest of the day
enters all my cravings!
                              I drink
five hundred times too much.
                                   I eat
like a bulemic trying to die.
                              Help me!

I know I'm not worth it,
but your generosity is so vast!

Let your sunlight shine on this piece of dung,
and dry it out, so I can be used for fuel
to warm and light up a bath-house.

Look on the terrible and stupid things I've done,
and cause herbs and eglantine to grow out of them.

The sun does this with the ground.
Think what glories God can make
from the fertilizer of sinning!

The Mouse continues to beg, *My Friend,*
I know I'm ugly to you.
                              I'm ugly to me!

I'm perfectly ugly!
                    But look, you'll be sad
when I die, won't you? You'll sit by my grave
and weep a little?
                    All I'm asking is,
be with me that little bit of time
while I'm still alive!
                    Now. I want you NOW!

A certain rich man was accustomed to honor a Sufi
by giving him pieces of silver.

"Would you like *one* piece of silver now,
O Lord of my Spirit, or *three* at breakfast
tomorrow morning?"
                    The Sufi answered,
"I love the half a coin that I have already in my hand
from yesterday more than the *promise* of a whole one
today, or the promise of a hundred tomorrow.
A Sufi is the child of *this* moment."

Back to the Mouse, who says,
                    The slap of Now
has cash in its hand. Give me slaps,
on the neck, anywhere!

Soul of my Soul of the Soul of a hundred universes,
be water in this Now-river. So jasmine flowers
will lift on the brim, and someone far off
can notice the flower-colors and know
there's water here.

"The sign is in the face." You can look at an orchard
and tell if it rained last night. That freshness
is the sign.

Again, the Mouse,
                    Friend, I'm made from the ground,
and for the ground. You're of the water.

I'm always standing on the bank calling to you.
Have mercy. I can't follow you into the water.
Isn't there some way we can be in touch?
A messenger? Some reminder?

The two Friends decided that the answer
was a long, *longing!* string, with one end tied
to the Mouse's foot and the other to the Frog's,
so that by pulling on it their secret connection
might be remembered and the two could meet,
as the Soul does with the Body.

The Frog-like Soul often escapes from the Body
and soars in the happy water. Then the Mouse-body
pulls on the string, and the Soul thinks,
                              Damn.
I have to go back on the riverbank and talk
with that scatterbrained Mouse!
                    You'll hear more about this
when you really wake up, on Resurrection Day!

So the Mouse and the Frog tied the string,
even though the Frog had a hunch some tangling
was to come.
                    Never ignore those intuitions.
When you feel some slight repugnance about doing something,
listen to it. These premonitions come from God.

Remember the story of the military elephant
who would not move toward the Kaaba.* Paralyzed

---

*The sacred black stone in Mecca

in that direction, yet swift if pointed toward Yemen.
It had some In-knowing from the Unseen.

So the Prophet Jacob, when his other sons wanted
to take Joseph out in the country for two days,
had a heart-sickness about their going, and it was true,
though Divine Destiny prevailed, despite his foreboding,
as It will.
                    It's not always a blind man
who falls in a pit. Sometimes it's one who can see.

A Holy One does sometimes fall,
but by that tribulation, he or she ascends,
escapes many illusions, escapes
conventional religion, escapes
being so bound to phenomena.

Think of how PHENOMENA come trooping
out of the Desert of Non-existence
into this materiality.
                        Morning and night,
they arrive in a long line and take over
from each other, "It's my turn now. Get out!"

A son comes of age, and the father packs up.
This place of phenomena is a wide exchange
of highways, with everything going all sorts
of different ways.
                    We seem to be sitting still,
but we're actually moving, and the Fantasies
of Phenomena are sliding through us
like ideas through curtains.
                            They go to the well
of deep love inside each of us.
They fill their jars there, and they leave.

There is a Source they come from,

and a fountain inside here.
                          Be generous.
Be grateful. Confess when you're not.

We can't know
what the Divine Intelligence
has in mind!

Who *am* I,
standing in the midst of this
thought-traffic?

(*Mathnawi*, VI, 2686-2786)

The Force of Friendship

A sea-cow, a dugong, finds a special pearl
and brings it up on land at night. By the light it gives off
the dugong can graze on hyacinths and lilies.

The excrement of the dugong is precious ambergris
because it eats such beauty. Anyone who feeds on Majesty
becomes eloquent. The bee, from mystic inspiration,
fills its rooms with honey.

So the dugong grazes at night in the pearl-glow.
Presently, a merchant comes and drops black loam
over the pearl, then hides behind a tree to watch.

The dugong surges about the meadow like a blind bull.
Twenty times it rushes at nothing, passing the mound
where the pearl is.
              So Satan couldn't see
the spirit-center inside Adam.
                   God says, *Descend*,
and a huge pearl from Aden gets buried under dirt.
The merchant knows,
              but the dugong doesn't.

Every clay-pile with a pearl inside
loves to be near any other clay-pile with a pearl,
but those without pearls cannot stand to be near
the hidden companionship.

Remember the mouse on the riverbank?
There's a love-string stretching into the water
hoping for the frog.
              Suddenly a raven grips the mouse
and flies off. The frog too, from the riverbottom,
with one foot tangled in invisible string,

follows, suspended in the air.
                              Amazed faces ask,
When did a raven ever go underwater
                              and catch a frog?

The frog answers,
            "This is the force of Friendship."
What draws Friends together
does not conform to Laws of Nature.
Form doesn't know about spiritual closeness.
If a grain of barley approaches a grain of wheat,
an ant must be carrying it. A black ant on black felt.
You can't see it, but if grains go toward each other,
it's there.
            A hand shifts our birdcages around.
Some are brought closer. Some move apart.
Do not try to reason it out. Be conscious
of who draws you and who not.

Gabriel was always there with Jesus, lifting him
above the dark-blue vault, the night-fortress world,
just as the raven of longing carries the flying frog.

(*Mathnawi*, VI, 2922-2973)

Moses and the Shepherd

Moses heard a shepherd on the road praying,
$$\text{"God,}$$
where are You? I want to help You, to fix Your shoes
and comb Your hair. I want to wash Your clothes
and pick the lice off. I want to bring You milk,
to kiss Your little hands and feet when it's time
for You to go to bed. I want to sweep Your room
and keep it neat. God, my sheep and goats
are Yours. All I can say, remembering You,
is *ayyyy* and *ahhhhhhhhh*."
$$\text{Moses could stand it no longer.}$$
"*Who* are you talking to?"
$$\text{"The One who made us,}$$
and made the earth and made the sky."
$$\text{"Don't talk about shoes}$$
and socks with God! And what's this with *Your little hands*
and feet? Such blasphemous familiarity sounds like
you're chatting with your uncles.
$$\text{Only something that grows}$$
needs milk. Only someone with feet needs shoes. Not God!
Even if you meant God's human representatives,
as when God said, 'I was sick, and you did not visit me,'
even then this tone would be foolish and irreverent.

Use appropriate terms. *Fatima* is a fine name
for a woman, but if you call a man *Fatima*,
it's an insult. Body-and-birth language
are right for us on this side of the river,
but not for addressing the Origin,
$$\text{not for Allah."}$$

The shepherd repented and tore his clothes and sighed
and wandered out into the desert.
$$\text{A sudden revelation}$$

came then to Moses. God's Voice:

*You have separated Me
from one of my own. Did you come as a Prophet to unite,
or to sever?*

*I have given each being a separate and unique way
of seeing and knowing and saying that knowledge.*

*What seems wrong to you is right for him.
What is poison to one is honey to someone else.*

*Purity and impurity, sloth and diligence in worship,
these mean nothing to Me.
I am apart from all that.
Ways of worshipping are not to be ranked as better
or worse than one another.
Hindus do Hindu things.
The Dravidian Muslims in India do what they do.
It's all praise, and it's all right.*

*It's not Me that's glorified in acts of worship.
It's the worshippers! I don't hear the words
they say. I look inside at the humility.*

*That broken-open lowliness is the Reality,
not the language! Forget phraseology.
I want burning, burning.
Be Friends
with your burning. Burn up your thinking
and your forms of expression!
Moses,
those who pay attention to ways of behaving
and speaking are one sort.
Lovers who burn
are another."*
Don't impose a property tax
on a burned out village. Don't scold the Lover.
The "wrong" way he talks is better than a hundred

"right" ways of others.
                    Inside the Kaaba
it doesn't matter which direction you point
your prayer rug!
                    The ocean diver doesn't need snowshoes!
The Love-Religion has no code or doctrine.
                                        Only God.
So the ruby has nothing engraved on it!
It doesn't need markings.
                    God began speaking
deeper mysteries to Moses. Vision and words,
which cannot be recorded here, poured into
and through him. He left himself and came back.
He went to Eternity and came back here.
Many times this happened.
                              It's foolish of me
to try and say this. If I did say it,
it would uproot our human intelligences.
It would shatter all writing pens.

Moses ran after the shepherd.
He followed the bewildered footprints,
in one place moving straight like a castle
across a chessboard. In another, sideways,
like a bishop.
                    Now surging like a wave cresting,
now sliding down like a fish,
                              with always his feet
making geomancy symbols in the sand,
                                        recording
his wandering state.
                    Moses finally caught up
with him.
                    "I was wrong. God has revealed to me
that there are no rules for worship.
                              Say whatever
and however your loving tells you to. Your sweet blasphemy

is the truest devotion. Through you a whole world
is freed.

      Loosen your tongue and don't worry what comes out.
It's all the Light of the Spirit."

                The shepherd replied,
"Moses, Moses,

          I've gone beyond even that.
You applied the whip and my horse shied and jumped
out of itself. The Divine Nature and my human nature
came together.

      Bless your scolding hand and your arm.
I can't say what has happened.

         What I'm saying now
is not my real condition. It can't be said."

The shepherd grew quiet.

      When you look in a mirror,
you see yourself, not the state of the mirror.
The fluteplayer puts breath into a flute,
and who makes the music? Not the flute.
The Fluteplayer!

      Whenever you speak praise
or thanksgiving to God, it's always like this
dear shepherd's simplicity.

      When you eventually see
through the veils to how things really are,
you will keep saying again
and again,

      "This is certainly not like
we thought it was!"

(*Mathnawi*, II, 1720-1796)

The Man Who Wanted to Learn
the Language of Animals

A young man asks Moses,

        "Teach me the language of animals.
Hopefully, listening to them will increase my Faith.
Human language seems to be mostly about getting food and fame.
It may be the animals have different concerns,
like what the moment of death means."

        Moses replies,
"This is a dangerous ability for you to want.
Wake yourself up in some other way. Try to learn
about God directly, not from other people's words,
not from books, not even from animal sounds."

Of course, that just makes the man want to learn
animal-language all the more.

"Moses, don't disappoint me in this. It's my last hope."

Moses asks God, "What shall I do? He's set on this one thing."

God says, "Teach him what he wants."

        "But this special power
is not suitable for him."

        Some devout people should stay weak
and poor. If they become successful in the world,
they abandon acts of self-denial and lose
their spiritual power.

        Numinous rose petals
aren't an appropriate diet for everyone.

God keeps saying though, "Give him what he's asking for.
He's free to choose."

        Choice is the salt on acts of worship.
If worship were compulsory, God would not be glorified.

"Put the sword in his hand, and let him become
either a Holy Warrior, or a thief. We have honored humankind
with the gift of free will."
                                        Everyone is half-honeybee, half-snak
Some eat herbs like a bee, and their spittle is medicine.
Others drink sherbet made from filthy water
and form venom in their mouths.
                                        All *bravos* and *well done's*
are because of mankind's having free will
and continuous watchful attention.
                                        Constant care and many small
deliberate choices are what is praised most in this world.
Negligent, self-indulgent people get put in jail,
and in there they become careful.
                                        Everyone in jail is prayerful
and ascetic, but when the power to choose is gone,
prayers become worth less.

                                        Hold on to your freedom
of choosing. It's the way God has honored you
as a Son of Adam.
                                        Once more, Moses,
                                                "What you want
will terrify you. I don't think you really want it."

"Yes I do. Teach me the language
of the dog and the chicken."

"It's done," says Moses.
                                        At daybreak, to test this out,
the young man stands in the doorway and watches a maid
shake out a tablecloth. A piece of bread from the night before
falls to the ground, and a rooster quickly pecks it up.

A dog standing nearby says, "This is not fair.
You eat grains of corn, which I can't. You enjoy barley

and all the rest. But that crust of bread!
                                        You *know*
how I love the greasy leftover scraps. You should have
let me have it. That was such a mean thing for you to do,
to scarf it up before I could get to it."
                                        The rooster,
"Do not complain. Be quiet. God will give you something
much better in place of this. The master's horse
is going to *die* tomorrow.
                            Tomorrow will be
a feast day for dogs!"

As soon as the young man, who owned the horse, hears this,
he leads the horse to market and sells it.

The next day the rooster runs off with the leftover bits
in the same way, and he and the dog have a similar discussion.

"You said the horse would die, but look,
the horse is gone. You lied."
                            "That horse *did* die,
but not here. The man sold the horse
so the loss would be someone else's.
                            Tomorrow though,
his *mule* will die."
                        Immediately the mule is sold,
and on the third day the dog:
                            "Liar, Prince of Liars,
where is my surprise banquet! Liar!"
                                        "I didn't lie.
The mule is dead, but, again, sold before it happened.
Tomorrow, I predict, and I'm always right, his slave will die,
and the next of kin will scatter out lots of bread
for beggars and dogs."
                            The man, of course, hears and happily
sells his dying slave for a fine profit.

He laughs,
"Three times, since I learned the language of dogs and chickens,
I have been saved from big losses."
The dog the next day,
"Rooster, what's your sniveling excuse this time?
Where are the bits and pieces you prophesied? *Nothing*
but lies roost in your nest, and nothing but lies
walk the dooryard."
                          "Not so, not so. Roosters are truthful,
like the priest that calls to prayers. We watch the sun
and carefully tell the time. In fact, we have the sun
inside us. You could turn a big basin over on top of me,
and I would still crow at dawn. Such inner-sun-knowers
are God's gift to mankind. We wake people up
and remind them of their prayers."
                                   The dog says nothing.
"I have another prediction for you.
                          Tomorrow the owner himself
will die, young man though he is, and his heir, in mourning,
will slaughter a cow. Some of the leavings will reach you,
pieces of roast meat and thin, hardcrusted bread,
just what you like!"

So the death of the horse and the mule and the slave
bring round the death of the man. He kept looking
for personal profit from his spiritual gift,
and so neglected his devotional work.

The One who acts without regard to getting anything back
is God. Or a Friend of God.
                          In this marketplace world
people sit on benches waiting to be paid.
                          The child won't give up
the onion in one hand until it has the apple tightly
in the other. Nobody says, "The Peace of God be with you,"
without some ulterior motive about making money.
                                   Very seldom

do you hear a true *Salaam*, one that means it. I listen
to hear God saying, *God's Peace be with you*,
but it's rare.

So the young man hears the rooster's prediction
and runs to Moses, "Save me, please save me."

Moses: "Why don't you sell yourself!
You've become so expert at avoiding loss.
Put the suffering off on someone else!
I saw this coming on the side of a brick.
But you couldn't see it if it were in your mirror."

"Moses, don't rub my nose in it. At least,
bless my Soul before I die."

                               With that, he began to feel
very sick. A basin is brought.

                               "Yes, try to vomit up
your profiteering!"

                     The man can't answer.
He is carried out by four men
with his legs folded across each other.

At dawn Moses gets up and prays, "Lord, forgive him
his impudence. No one who can't keep his mouth shut
is fit to learn the secrets of the Unseen.

                            Only seabirds
live on the Ocean. This one is definitely a land-bird.
He's sinking. Help him."

"Would you like me to raise him from the dead? For you,
Moses, I would raise *everyone* from the dead!"

                             "No. Dying
is proper for this world. Give him, and everyone,
the mercy of Faith in the next world."

                         And it was done.

I tell you this story to remind you
that the loss of the body, and the loss
of material wealth is good for your spirit.

Buy discipline and service to others with your life,
and if discipline comes without your asking for it,
bow your head and be grateful.
                              When that happens,
God is paying special attention to you,
                              is holding you close,
and whispering in your ear
                    the original word,
                                          BE!

(*Mathnawi*, III, 3266-3438)

The Lost Camel

You've lost your camel, my friend,
and everyone's giving you advice.

You don't know where your camel is,
but you do know these casual directions
are wrong. Even someone who hasn't lost a camel,
who's never even owned a camel, gets in on
the excitement, "Yes, I've lost my camel too.
A big reward for whoever finds it."
                              He says this
in order to be part-owner of your camel when you find it.
If you say to anyone's suggestion, "I don't think so,"
the imitator says the same thing immediately.
When good information comes, you know it right away,
but not the imitator.
                    That bit of information
is medicine to you. It gives color to your face
and strength to your body. Your eyes brighten.
Your feet get lively and agile. You say,
                              "Thank You,
my Friend, this Truth you give feels like freedom to me.
Please go in front. Be the leader! You have the scent
of my camel better than I do."
                              But the imitator doesn't feel
the intensity of those clues. He hears your wild outcries,
though, and gets some inkling of what it might be like to be close
to finding a lost camel.

He has, indeed, lost a camel,
but he doesn't know it!

Wanting and imitating someone else's wanting
has blinded him. But as he follows along in the searching,

calling out what the others call out,
                              suddenly he sees
his own camel browsing there, the one
he didn't know he'd lost.

Only then, does he become a seeker.
He turns aside and goes by himself toward his camel.

The sincere one asks, "Why have you left my search?"

"Up until now I was a fake. I was flattering you,
because I wanted to be part of your glory.
Now that I've separated myself from you,
I am more truly connected to you.
I know what you're doing. Before,
I was stealing camel-descriptions from you.

When my spirit saw its own camel, that seeing
filled everything. Now all my insincerity
and copycat words have changed to virtues.
They brought me *here*! I was sowing my own seed,
though I thought I was working for nothing.

Like a thief I crept and entered a house,
and it was my own home!"

Be fiery, cold one, so heat can come.
Endure rough surfaces that smooth you.

The subject of all this is not *two camels*.
There's only one lost camel,
but language has difficulty saying that.

Muhammed said, "Whoever knows God, stammers."
Speaking is like an astrolabe pointing at the sky.
How much, really, can such a device know?

Especially of that Other Sky,
to which this one is a piece of straw?
That Other Sun, in which this is a fleck of dust?

(Mathnawi, II, 2973–3015)

The Mouse and the Camel

A mouse caught hold of a camel's leading-rope
in his two forelegs and walked off with it,
imitating the camel-drivers.
                          The camel went along,
letting the mouse feel heroic.
                          "Enjoy yourself,"
he thought. "I have something to teach you, presently."

They came to the edge of a great river.
The mouse was dumbfounded.
                          "What are you waiting for?
Step forward into the river. You are my leader.
Don't stop here."
                          "I'm afraid of being drowned."

The camel walked into the water. "It's only
just above the knee."
                          "*Your* knee! Your knee
is a hundred times over my head!"
                          "Well, maybe you shouldn't
be leading a camel. Stay with those like yourself.
A mouse has nothing really to say to a camel."

"Would you help me get across?"

"Get up on my hump. I am made
to take hundreds like you across."

You are not a prophet, but go humbly on the Way of the Prophets,
and you can arrive where they are. Don't try to steer the boat.
Don't open a shop by yourself. Listen. Keep silent.
You are not God's mouthpiece. Try to be an ear,
and if you do speak, ask for explanations.

The source of your arrogance and anger is your lust
and the rootedness of that is in your habits.

Someone who makes a habit of eating clay
gets mad when you try to keep him from it.
Being a leader can also be a poisonous habit,
so that when someone questions your authority,
you think, "He's trying to take over."
You may respond courteously, but inside you rage.

Always check your inner state
with the Lord of your Heart.
Copper doesn't know it's copper,
until it's changed to gold.

Your loving doesn't know its Majesty,
until it knows its helplessness.

(*Mathnawi*, II, 3436-3474)

The Servant Who Loved His Prayers

At dawn a certain rich man
wanted to go to the steambaths.
He woke his servant, Sunqur,

        "Ho! Get moving! Get the basin
and the towels and the clay for washing
and let's go to the baths."

Sunqur immediately collected what was needed,
and they set out side by side along the road.

As they passed the mosque, the call to prayer sounded.
Sunqur loved his five-times prayer.

        "Please, master,
rest on this bench for a while that I may recite Sura 98,
which begins,

        'You who treat your slave with kindness.'"

The master sat on the bench outside while Sunqur went in.
When prayers were over, and the priest and all the worshippers
had left, still Sunqur remained inside. The master waited
and waited. Finally he yelled into the mosque,

        "Sunqur,
why don't you come out?"

        "I can't. This Clever One
won't let me. Have a little more patience.
I hear you out there."

        Seven times the master waited,
and then shouted. Sunqur's reply was always the same,
"Not yet. He won't let me come out yet."

        "But there's no one
in there but you. Everyone else has left.
Who makes you sit still so long?"

"The One who keeps me in here is the One who keeps you out there.

The Same who will not let you in will not let me out."

The Ocean will not allow its fish out of itself.
Nor does it let land animals in
where the subtle and delicate fish move.

The land creatures lumber along on the ground.
No cleverness can change this. There's only one
Opener for the lock of these matters.

Forget your figuring. Forget your self. Listen to your Friend.
When you become totally obedient to That One,
you'll be free.

(*Mathnawi*, III, 3055-3076)

Two Kinds of Intelligence

There are two kinds of intelligence: One acquired,
as a child in school memorizes facts and concepts
from books and from what the teacher says,
collecting information from the traditional sciences
as well as from the new sciences.

With such intelligence you rise in the world.
You get ranked ahead or behind others
in regard to your competence in retaining
information. You stroll with this intelligence
in and out of fields of knowledge, getting always more
marks on your preserving tablets.

There is another kind of tablet, one
already completed and preserved inside you.
A spring overflowing its springbox. A freshness
in the center of the chest. This other intelligence
does not turn yellow or stagnate. It's fluid,
and it doesn't move from outside to inside
through the conduits of plumbing-learning.

This second knowing is a fountainhead
from within you, moving out.

(Mathnawi, IV, 1960-1968)

Where Are We?

An invisible bird flies over,
but casts a quick shadow.

What is the body? That shadow of a shadow
of your love, that somehow contains
the entire universe.

A man sleeps heavily,
though something blazes in him like the sun,
like a magnificent fringe sewn up under the hem.

He turns under the covers.
Any image is a lie:

> A clear red stone tastes sweet.

> You kiss a beautiful mouth, and a key
> turns in the lock of your fear.

> A spoken sentence sharpens to a fine edge.

> A mother dove looks for her nest,
> asking where, *ku*? Where, *ku*?

Where the lion lies down.
Where any man or woman goes to cry.
Where the sick go when they hope to get well.

Where a wind lifts that helps with winnowing,
and the same moment, sends a ship on its way.

Where anyone says *Only God Is Real.*
Ya Hu! Where beyond *where.*

A bright weaver's shuttle flashes back and forth,
east-west, *Where-are-we? Ma ku? Maku.*
like the sun saying *Where are we?*
as it weaves with the asking.

(*Mathnawi*, VI, 3288-3295, 3306-3322)

(Note: In Persian the imagery of the last stanza contains a complex pun.
Maku means "a weaver's shuttle." *Ma ku* means, "Where are we?"

Hu is the pronoun of Divine Presence.)

Imra'u 'l-Qays

Imra'u 'l-Qays, King of the Arabs,
was very handsome, and a poet, full of love-songs.

Women loved him desperately.
Everyone loved him, but there came one night
an experience that changed him completely.
He left his kingdom and his family.
He put on dervish robes and wandered
from one weather, one landscape, to another.

Love dissolved his king-self
and led him to Tabuk, where he worked for a time
making bricks. Someone told the King of Tabuk
about Imra'u 'l-Qays, and that king went to visit him
at night.
         "King of the Arabs, handsome Joseph of this age,
ruler of two empires, one composed of territories,
and the other of the beauty of women,
if you would consent to stay with me,
I would be honored. You abandon kingdoms,
because you want more
than kingdoms."

The King of Tabuk went on like this,
praising Imra'u 'l-Qays, and talking theology
and philosophy. Imra'u 'l-Qays kept silent.
Then suddenly he leaned and whispered something
in the second king's ear, and that second, that
second king became a wanderer too.

They walked out of town hand in hand.
No royal belts, no thrones.

This is what love does and continues to do.

It tastes like honey to adults and milk to children.
Love is the last thirty pound bale.
When you load it on, the boat tips over.

So they wandered around China like birds
pecking at bits of grain. They rarely spoke
because of the dangerous seriousness
of the secret they knew.

That love-secret spoken pleasantly, or in irritation,
severs a hundred thousand heads in one swing.
A Love-lion grazes in the soul's pasture,
while the scimitar of this secret approaches.
It's a killing better than any living.

All that world-power wants, really,
is this weakness.

So these kings talked in low tones,
and carefully. Only God knows what they said.

They used unsayable words. Bird-language.
But some people have imitated them, learned
a few bird-calls, and gotten prestigious.

(*Mathnawi*, VI, 3986-4010)

The Barking of Invisible Puppies

There are many impudent hypocrites
who see nothing of the way of holy men
but their *suf*, their white woolen robes.
Each one picks up a stick and says, "I am Moses,"
or walks among the gullible saying, "I am Jesus."
Pity the day when their sincerity is tested.
Ask what external forms mean. What you want and get,
you lose. You've heard some words, and now you're an expert
at repeating them. A parrot sees its own reflection in a mirror.
The parrot-teacher is behind the mirror, talking low.
The parrot thinks the parrot facing it is talking,
thinks it's learning human speech from one of its own.
It *can* and does speak, word for word, what it hears,
though it stays ignorant of meaning and mystery.
Thus a disciple sometimes sees himself mirrored in a teacher's body
and doesn't see or hear what's behind the mirror of discourse.
He thinks a man is talking. He learns words as people
learn birdcalls with their mouths and throats,
but they don't know what the birds are saying.
From the pulpit and in the meeting hall, many repeat
what dervishes say. Sometimes it's just a formality,
and sometimes a great mercy has shown them a Truth.

During a *chilla*, a forty-day retreat, a certain man
dreams that he sees a bitch-dog pregnant with puppies
coming along a road. He hears the barking of puppies!
Invisible puppies inside the womb, *barking*!
The man is astonished. He wakes up, still amazed.
No one can untangle this knot except the presence of God.
He prays, *Because of this puzzle in my head,*
I can't do the zikr as I should. Untie my wings,
so I can fly back to the orchard. Immediately a voice:
"The pregnant dog with the barking puppies
is an emblem of idle talk about spiritual matters.

Some people speak before they're born. Still blind,
they act as though they see. The yelp of a puppy
in the womb is not to keep watch, or to start game,
or for food. It is the speech of a man who wants
spiritual eminence without the reality.
The barking is his nonsense. He points
to what he doesn't see. He wants to buy things.
He doesn't care how he himself has been bought by God.
He makes love to two sweethearts. Actually he hasn't enough
to buy half a horseshoe, while those who listen quietly
to him are offering amethysts and rubies.
His desire is for influence and power, blind and rushing
to sell to anyone. Whereas patience and self-denial
try to find the buyer that has already bought them, the owner."

(*Mathnawi*, V, 1423-1472)

Who Makes These Changes?

Who makes these changes?
I shoot an arrow right.
It lands left.
I ride after a deer and find myself
chased by a hog.
I plot to get what I want
and end up in prison.
I dig pits to trap others
and fall in.

I should be suspicious
of what I want.

(*Mathnawi*, VI, 3682-3687)

Why Wine is Forbidden

When the Prophet's ray of Intelligence
struck the dimwitted man he was with,
the man got very happy, and talkative.

Soon, he began unmannerly raving.
This is the problem with a selflessness
that comes quickly,
                              as with wine.
If the wine-drinker
has a deep gentleness in him,
he will show that,
                              when drunk.
But if he has hidden anger and arrogance,
those appear,
                              and since most people do,
wine is forbidden to everyone.

(*Mathnawi*, IV, 2154-2158)

On Resurrection Day

On Resurrection Day your body testifies against you.
Your hand says, "I stole money."
Your lips, "I said meanness."
Your feet, "I went where I shouldn't."
Your genitals, "Me too."

They will make your praying sound hypocritical.
Let the body's doings speak openly now,
without your saying a word,
as a student's walking behind a teacher
says, "This one knows more clearly
than I the way."

(*Mathnawi*, V, 2211-2220)

A Tenth of the Harvest, a Tenth of the Flour, a Tenth of the Bread

In the village of Zarwan near the border of Yemen
there was a good man, who took care of the poor
and the troubled. They came to him, and he gave
without calling attention to his giving, a tenth
of his harvest of corn and wheat, and a tenth
after the threshing. When it was ground into flour,
he gave a tenth of that, and also a tenth of the bread.
Anything that grew on his land he tithed four times.
He instructed his sons, "After I am gone, continue
to do the same. This produce is not our doing.
We must give to what gave." A good farmer
sows back the major part of his seed.
He has no doubt that it will grow again.
He generously moves his hand back and forth.

A good shoemaker buys more hides and morocco
with the profits left over. He says, "This is my livelihood.
It must keep flowing, untying the knot."
He is generous to that which gave his income.
The soil and the leather are images of another source.
When you sow into *that*, a thousand blessednesses
grow from one seed. Let's say you've sown
a seed recently. I'm guessing that you have.
If nothing happens in two or three years,
you might put your hand to your head in prayer.
That hand on your head is what you were looking for.
Find ecstasy within, not in wine and hashish.
Find wealth *there*, not from relatives.
You're looking at pictures. Turn to the painter.

If friends become angry at you, be happy
that what will happen at the end happens now.
You bought damaged goods, and you were going home pleased,

but now you see what they are. Your companion
shows an itch of hatred, and jealousy shoots out
at you. Thank God you didn't remain and get rotten
in that sack. Now you can leave and look for a true friend.
You found the tumor in time. People are cruel and resentful
to you, so that you may turn away. Be thankful.
There is One whose harshness is better
than the kindness of the faithful.

Owners of large granaries, sow your wheat
back into the ground, to keep it safe from thieves
and weevils! Partridges are not meant to prey on hawks.
You shouldn't be afraid of the threat of poverty.
So the father sowed the seed back into his sons,
but with them it didn't work. There are those
who won't hear. Mountains move, but sometimes
nothing affects an unbeliever. He keeps saying *I*,
or *we*, for the center of his being, which is,
as the *Qur'an* says, a *No*, harder than stone.

(*Mathnawi*, V, 1473-1536)

You Are Not a Single YOU

You're a common rhyme-word now,
dependent on some other for your emotional force,
but real life will come.

As when a baby stops nursing and grows interested
in solid food. As when seeds break open in the ground
and act differently.
                        There is a hidden love-center
in human beings that you will discover and savor
and nourish yourself with. That will be your food.

There's a way of going that's like the stars.
                                            No,
even freer than they are, completely unconditioned,
unlocated, unpathed. A journey without a sky!

You came from Non-existence into being.
How did that happen? Tell me about it!
You were a little drunk when you arrived,
so you can't remember exactly?
                        I'll give you
some secret hints. Let your mind go, and be mindful.
Close your ears, and listen.
                        But maybe I shouldn't tell,
if you're not ripe. You're still in early Spring.
July hasn't happened yet in you.
                        This world is a tree,
and we are green, half-ripe fruit on it.
We hold tight to the limbs, because we know
we're not ready to be taken into the palace.

When we mature and sweeten,
                        we'll feel ashamed

at having clung so clingingly.
                                        To hold fast
is a sure sign of unripeness.
                                        To drink and enjoy
blood is fine for an embryo.

More needs to be said on this, but the Holy Spirit
will tell it to you when I'm not here.
                                        You'll tell it
to *yourself*. Not I, or some other "I," You
who are Me!
                        As when you fall asleep and go
from the presence of your self to the Presence
of your Self. You hear That One and you think,
"Someone must have communicated telepathically
in my sleep."
                        You are not a single You,
good Friend, you are a Sky and an Ocean,
a tremendous YHUUUUUU, a nine hundred times huge
drowning place for all your hundreds of you's.

What are these terms *wakefulness* and *sleep*?
Don't answer. Let God answer.
Don't speak, so the Speakers can.
Not a word, so Sun-Light can say
what has never been in a book, or said.
Don't *try* to put it into words,
and the Spirit will do that through you,
in spite of you,
                        beside you,
                                        among you.
Stop swimming so hard,
                                        and climb in the boat
with Noah.

(*Mathnawi*, III, 1283-1307)

As the Orchard Is with the Rain

Don't be like Canaan, Noah's son,
who wouldn't get in the ark.

He was swimming and saying, "I hate my father.
I won't use that boat."

Noah called, "Come. Sit in this
that I've made, or you'll drown."
                                    "No!
I've learned how to swim on my own.
I've lit my candle from a flame other than yours."

"Don't do it, Canaan. This flood extinguishes
all candles of human ingenuity. Only God's candle
can make it through these waves. Stop
your arrogant claims, and get in."
                                    "No!
I can make it to that mountaintop.
I'll be safe there."
                        "Mountains are just bits of straw
in this storm. There's no refuge
except with God's Beloved."
                                "When have I ever
taken your advice? Your words mean nothing to me,
in either world! Leave me alone!"
                                    "O little father,"
continued Noah, "don't do this! This is no time
for self-conceit. Until now you've shown contempt
for me and for God. Now God is showing disdain.
Be careful! Your disdain means nothing to God.

God is not begotten. God has said, 'Young man,
don't strut . . . Old man, don't be proud . . .
Husband, I have no lust . . . Lady, I am not coy . . .

All that helps in My Presence is utter
and complete helplessness.'"
                              Canaan replied,
"Father, you've been saying this for years.
You must be insane to think I'll listen now.
I have my own wisdom. I don't need
your tiresome preaching."
                              "But what harm will it do,
my son, to listen just a little longer?"

So they were calling back and forth, with Noah
never relenting in his admonishments
to his son.
              Suddenly a wave came
that buried Canaan and tore him to pieces.

"My Lord and my King," said Noah,
"You have taken this one from me, yet many times
you promised that my family would be saved."
God answered,
              "Canaan was not one of yours.
Can't you see that he is blue, and you are white!"

When a tooth is rotten, pull it out.
It's not a tooth any more. If you don't,
the rest of your body will be miserable.
Be rid of it, even though it was once yours."

And Noah replied,
              "I am rid of everything
but your Essence. You know how I am with You,
as the orchard is with the rain, and twenty times
that! Living in You, rejoicing in You,
like a beggar receiving all he needs directly
from Wealth itself, with no one's hand in between.
Not united, not separated. Perfection. No!

51

No qualities, no description. No cause.

Before the flood and after it, every word
I say is of You, in You, from You, as a woman
speaks night and day with the ruins of her Beloved,
where now she lives in perpetual conversation.

A lover seems to be facing wreckage,
but I hear the song of praise coming back
from the ruins as an echo of Your Name.
I love Your Name. I love it doubled.
That's why the prophets love the mountains,
because of the echoes. Little low hills
won't do. They don't send Your Name back
to me when I say it."
                                "Noah, Noah," said God,
I will raise Canaan and all these others
from the dead if you wish. I don't want you
to grieve."
                        "No. Drown me too. Keep drowning me
every moment. Your will is my joy. I carry it
with me as my Soul.
                                I only see You. I am in love
with whatever Your Creating does. You make
happiness, and I'm grateful. You make
disaster, and I'm patient.
                                Anyone who loves
Your making is full of Glory. Anyone who loves
what You have made is not a true believer."

(*Mathnawi*, III, 1310-1361)

When We Pray Alone

We are brought thick desserts, and we rarely refuse them.
We worship devoutly when we're with others.
Hours we sit,
                    though we get up quickly,
after a few minutes, when we pray alone.
We hurry down the gullet of our wantings.

But these qualities can change,
as minerals in the ground rise inside trees
and become tree, as a plant faces an animal
and enters the animal, so a human
can put down the heavy
body-baggage and
be light.

(*Mathnawi*, VI, 118-128)

One Who Wraps Himself

God called the Prophet Muhammed *Muzzammil,*
"The One Who Wraps Himself,"
                              and said,
"Come out from under your cloak, you so fond
of hiding and running away.
                              Don't cover your face.
The world is a reeling, drunken body, and You
are its intelligent head.
                              Don't hide the candle
of your clarity. Stand up and burn
through the night, my Prince.
                              Without your Light
a great Lion is held captive by a rabbit!

Be the Captain of the Ship,
Mustafa, my Chosen One,
my expert guide.
                    Look how the caravan of civilization
has been ambushed.
                    Fools are everywhere in charge.
Do not practice solitude like Jesus. Be *in*
the assembly,
              and take charge of it.
                              As the bearded griffon,
the *Humay,* lives on Mt. Qaf because he's native to it,
so You
          should live most naturally out in public
and be a communal teacher of souls."

(*Mathnawi,* IV, 1453-1463)

Dance with the Bandage Torn Off

Dance, when you're broken open.
Dance, if you've torn the bandage off.
Dance in the middle of the fighting.
Dance in your blood.
Dance, when you're perfectly free.

Struck, the dancers hear a tambourine inside them,
as a wave turns to foam on its very top, begin.

Maybe you don't hear that tambourine,
or the tree leaves clapping time.

Close the ears on your head
that listen mostly to lies and cynical jokes.
There are other things to hear and see:
dance-music and a brilliant city
inside the Soul.
                    God said of Muhammed,
He is an ear.
                He was wholly ear and eye,
and we are refreshed and fed by that,
as an infant boy is at his mother's breast.

(*Mathnawi*, III, 95-103)

Send the Chaperones Away

Inside me a hundred beings
are putting their fingers to their lips and saying,
"That's enough for now. Shhhhh." Silence
is an ocean. Speech
is a river.

When the Ocean is searching for you, don't walk
to the language-river. Listen to the Ocean,
and bring your talky business
to an end.

Traditional words are just babbling
in that Presence, and babbling is a substitute
for sight. When you sit down beside your Beloved,
send the chaperones away, the old women
who brought you together.

When you are mature and with your love,
the love-letters and matchmakers
seem irritating.
You might read those letters,
but only to teach beginners about love. One who sees
grows silent. When you're with one of those,
be still and quiet, unless he asks you
to talk. Then draw the words out
as I do this poem with Husam,
the Radiance of God.
I try to stop talking,
but he makes me continue. Husam, if you are in
the Vision, why do you want me to say *words*?

Maybe it's like the poet Abu Nuwas,
who said in Arabic,
Pour me some wine,

and talk *to me about the wine.*
The Cup is at my mouth,
but my ear interrupts,
"I want some."

O Ear, what you get is the heat.
You turn red with this wine.
But the ear says,
"I want more than that!"

(*Mathnawi*, IV, 2061-2063, 2065-2080)

What Wine Is to a Lover

When a gnostic says, "wine,"
what does he mean?

How does he make a liquid
refer to *that*!

If you only know one kind of wine,
you will not know the Other, until a poet
and the Juice of Generosity collaborate
to make something new.

Young lovers like to drink red wine
and listen to love songs,
                              but there's another
Lover, another Wine, another Lovesong,
another Tavern.
                    Hand me, says the mystic poet
to the One he can't see, *Your Cup.*
You are my face. No wonder I can't see You.
You are the intricate workings of my mind.
You are the big artery in my neck.
When I call out in the desert, O God,
I'm only pretending, to distract the others,
so they won't notice Who sits beside me.

(*Mathnawi*, VI, 657-669)

Sheikh Kharraqani and His Wretched Wife

Don't look at me.
Fall into the safety of God.
I'm already drowned.
Do I have a beard?
I can't remember.

Rescue this man from his mustache,
curling so proudly, while inside he tears
his hair. Married to God, married
to God, but pretending not!

We see distinctly what this imposture
becomes in a hundred years. A sheikh
looks into a chunk of iron like it's a mirror.
What this bushy-bearded man does not discover in his house
a boy could find so easily.

Dive into the Ocean.
You're caught in your own pretentious beard
like something you didn't eat.
You're not garbage! Pearls want to be
like you. You should be with them
where waves and fish and pearls and seaweed and wind
are all one. No linking, no hierarchy,
no distinctions, no perplexed wondering, no speech.
Beyond describing.

Either stay here and talk or go there and be silent.
Or do both, by turns.
With those who see double, talk doubletalk.
Make noise, beat a drum, think of metaphors!
With Friends, say only mystery.
Near roses, sing.

With deceptive people, cover the jar, and shield it.
But be calm with those in duality.
Speak sweetly and reasonably.
Patience polishes and purifies.

Here's the story of a man looking for Sheikh Kharraqani.

A certain dervish goes out from Talaqan, over the mountains
and through a long valley. The injuries and troubles he suffered
deserve mention, but I'll make it short. The young man
arrives at the Sheikh's house and knocks.
The Sheikh's wife sticks her head out, "What do you want!"

"I come with the intention of seeing the Sheikh."

"Oho," laughs the wife, "look at his Reverence! Was there
nothing to do where you live that you came on such an idle,
sight-seeing expedition? Do you hate your hometown? Or maybe
Satan led you here by the nose?" I won't tell you
all she said.

"Still, I would like to see the Sheikh."

"Better you should turn around and go home. Hundreds of your kind
have come like Israelites to rub their hands on this arrogant
gold calf, parasite, licker-of-platters-on-the-floor,
heavy-slumbering good-for-nothing. They say, O,
this is ecstasy, O. They forget any real religious ceremony
and ritual prayers."

The young man could stand it no more. "What is this? I've been
ambushed by a night-patrol in full daylight! Your blitherings
try to keep me from the presence of a holy man,
but I know what light led me here, the same that turned
the golden calf into words in a sacred story. A saint
is a theatre where the qualities of God can be seen.

Don't try to keep me out. Puff on this candle,
and your face will get burned! Rather try blowing out
the sun, or fitting a muzzle on the sea!
Old bats like you often dream that their cave-dark
is everywhere, but it's not.

My determination to be in that Presence is quick and constant.
You won't stop or slow me.
A revealer of mystery and that which is revealed
are the same. Seed, sowing, growing, harvest, One Presence.
The husk, old hag of a nagging world,
should bow to that.

Hallaj said, *I am God*, and lived it out.
What happens when the *I* disappears?
What's left after *not*?

Whoever scoffs at these questions and the experiences
they point to, his arrogant spit comes back in his face.
There is no spitting on the way we're on.
Rain itself turns to spit on those who mock
and casually show disrespect to saints."

With that he left the doorway and walked about
asking in the town. Finally someone, "The Qutb
is in the forest collecting wood." The young dervish
ran toward the forest but with a doubt,
"Why should such a Sheikh have such a woman
for a wife, such an opposite, such a Neanderthal!
God forgive my impugning. Who am I
to judge?" But the question remained.

How could a Teacher lie with that woman!
Can a Guide agree with a thief?

Suddenly Sheikh Kharraqani appears, riding a lion,

firewood stacked behind him. His whip,
a live serpent. Every Sheikh rides a fierce lion,
whether you see it or not. Know this
with your other eyes: There are thousands of lions
under your teacher's thighs and all of them
stacked with wood!

Kharraqani knew the problem and immediately began to answer,
"Well, it's not out of desire that I put up with her!
Don't think that. It's not her perfume
or her bright-colored clothes. Enduring her
public disdain has made me strong and patient.
She is my practice. Nothing can be clear
without a polar opposite present. Two banners,
one black, one white, and between them
something gets settled. Between Pharoah
and Moses, the Red Sea.

You consider issues, but not deeply enough.
Your spring is frozen. Faith is a flowing.
Don't try to forge cold iron.
Study David, the ironsmith, and dancer, and musician.
Move into the sun. You're wrapped in fantasy
and inner mumbling. When spirit enters,
a man begins to wander freely, escaped and overrunning
through the garden plants, spontaneous and soaking in."

Now a miracle story . . .

(*Mathnawi*, VI, 2019-2190)

Dig a Hole in This Book

Maybe you can't drink the entire Oxus River
but don't deny you're thirsty!

You want a spirit-drenching?
Dig a hole in this book, the *Mathnawi*,
this island. Make holes,
so the ocean can flow up through.
Dig and make it porous
until it's all seawater.

Wind moves word-leaves off the surface,
showing one-color, clearness.

Beneath you, coral branches,
and ocean-peaches!

When the *Mathnawi* sinks, with your digging,
it loses its words. Speaker, listener, language.
Bread-giver, bread-taker, bread.
The categories dissolve
into One Water.

(*Mathnawi*, VI, 66-73)

The Naked Sun

Those who live in Union
become pregnant with the feelings and words
of invisible forms!
                        Their amazed mouths
open. Their eyes withdraw.

Children are born of that illumination.
We say "born," but that's not right.
It only points to a new understanding.

Be quiet and let the Master of Speech talk.
Don't try to dress up your own nightingale-song
to sell to this Rose! Be all ear.

This pregnancy!
                        So subtle and delicious,
the way ice in July reminds us of winter,
the way fruit in January tells of summer
generosity,
                        that's how the naked Sun
embraces all the orchard-brides at once.

(*Mathnawi*, VI, 1810-1822)

Jesus on the Lean Donkey

Jesus on the lean donkey,
this is an emblem of how the rational intellect
should control the animal-soul.

                              Let your Spirit
be strong like Jesus.

                    If that part becomes weak,
then the worn-out donkey grows to a dragon.

Be grateful when what seems unkind
comes from a wise person.

                              Once, a holy man,
riding his donkey, saw a snake crawling into
a sleeping man's mouth! He hurried, but he couldn't
prevent it. He hit the man several blows with his club.

The man woke terrified and ran beneath an apple tree
with many rotten apples on the ground.

                              "Eat!
You miserable wretch! Eat."

                              "Why are you doing this to me?"
"Eat more, you fool."

                    "I've never seen you before!
Who are you? Do you have some inner quarrel with my soul?"

The wise man kept forcing him to eat, and then he ran him.
For hours he whipped the poor man and made him run.
Finally, at nightfall, full of rotten apples,
fatigued, bleeding, he fell

                              and vomited everything,
the good and the bad, the apples and the snake.

When he saw that ugly snake
come out of himself, he fell on his knees
before his assailant.

                    "Are you Gabriel? Are you God?

I bless the moment you first noticed me. I was dead
and didn't know it. You've given me a new life.
Everything I've said to you was stupid!
I didn't know."
                          "If I had explained what I was doing,
you might have panicked and died of fear.
Muhammed said,
                          'If I described the enemy that lives
inside men, even the most courageous would be paralyzed. No one
would go out, or do any work. No one would pray or fast,
and all power to change would fade
from human beings,'
                          so I kept quiet
while I was beating you, that like David
I might shape iron, so that, impossibly,
I might put feathers back into a bird's wing.

God's Silence is necessary, because of humankind's
faintheartedness. If I had told you about the snake,
you wouldn't have been able to eat, and if
you hadn't eaten, you wouldn't have vomited.

I saw your condition and drove my donkey hard
into the middle of it, saying always under my breath,
'Lord, make it easy on him.' I wasn't permitted
to tell you, and I wasn't permitted to stop
beating you!"
                          The healed man, still kneeling,
"I have no way to thank you for the quickness
of your wisdom and the strength
of your guidance.
                          God will thank you."

(*Mathnawi*, II, 1858-1860, 1878-1929)

The Snake-Catcher and the Frozen Snake

Listen to this, and hear the mystery inside:
A snake-catcher went into the mountains to find a snake.

He wanted a friendly pet, and one that would amaze
audiences, but he was looking for a reptile, something
that has no knowledge of friendship.
                                        It was winter.
In the deep snow he saw a frighteningly huge dead snake.
He was afraid to touch it, but he did.
In fact, he dragged the thing into Baghdad,
hoping people would pay to see it.
                                This is how foolish
we've become! A human being is a mountain range!
Snakes are fascinated by *us*! Yet we sell ourselves
to look at a dead snake.
                        We are like beautiful satin
used to patch burlap. "Come see the dragon I killed,
and hear the adventures!" That's what he announced,
and a large crowd came,
                        but the dragon was not dead,
just dormant! He set up his show at a crossroads.
The ring of gawking rubes got thicker, everybody
on tiptoe, men and women, noble and peasant, all
packed together unconscious of their differences.
It was like the Resurrection!

He began to unwind the thick ropes and remove
the cloth coverings he'd wrapped it so well in.

Some little movement.
                        The hot Iraqi sun had woken
the terrible life. The people nearest started screaming.
Panic! The dragon tore easily and hungrily
loose, killing many instantly.
                            The snake-catcher stood there,

frozen. "What have I brought out of the mountains?" The snake braced against a post and crushed the man and consumed him.

The snake is your animal-soul. When you bring it
into the hot air of your wanting-energy, warmed
by that and by the prospect of power and wealth,
it does massive damage.

Leave it in the snow mountains.
Don't expect to oppose it with quietness
and sweetness and wishing.

The *nafs* don't respond to those,
and they can't be killed. It takes a Moses to deal
with such a beast, to lead it back, and make it lie down
in the snow. But there was no Moses then.
Hundreds of thousands died.

(*Mathnawi*, III, 976-977, 993-1007, 1029-1067)

A Basket of Fresh Bread

The Prophet Muhammed said,
                    "There is no better companion
on this Way than what you do. Your actions
will be your best Friend, or if you're cruel and selfish,
your actions will be a poisonous snake that lives
in your grave."
                    But tell me, can you do the Good Work
without a teacher? Can you even know what it is
without the Presence of a Master? Notice how
the lowest livelihood requires some instruction.

First comes knowledge, then the doing of the job.
And much later, perhaps after you're dead,
something grows from what you've done.

Look for help and guidance in whatever craft
you're learning. Look for a generous teacher,
one who has absorbed the tradition he's in.

Look for pearls in oyster shells.
Learn technical skill from a craftsman.

Whenever you meet genuine spiritual teachers,
be gentle and polite and fair with them.
Ask them questions, and be eager
for the answers. Never condescend.

If a master tanner wears an old, threadbare smock,
that doesn't diminish his mastery.

If a fine blacksmith works at the bellows
in a patched apron, it doesn't affect
how he bends the iron.
                    Strip away
your pride, and put on humble clothes.

If you want to learn theory, *talk*
with theoreticians. That way is oral.

When you learn a craft, practice it.
That learning comes through the *hands*.

If you want dervishood, spiritual poverty,
and emptiness, you must be Friends with a Sheikh.
Talking about it, reading books, and doing practices
don't help. Soul receives from soul that Knowing.

The mystery of spiritual emptiness may be living
in a pilgrim's heart, and yet the knowing of it
may not yet be his.

Wait for the illuminating openness,
as though your chest were filling with Light,
as when God said,

> *Did We not expand you?*

> *(Qur'an*, XCIV, 1)

Don't look for it outside yourself.
You are the source of milk. Don't milk others!

There is a milk-fountain inside you.
Don't walk around with an empty bucket.
You have a channel into the Ocean, and yet
you ask for water from a little pool.

Beg for that love-expansion. Meditate only
on THAT. The *Qur'an* says,

> *And He is with you*

> (LVII, 4)

There is a basket of fresh bread on your head, and yet
you go door to door asking for crusts.

Knock on your inner door. No other.

Sloshing kneedeep in fresh riverwater, yet
you keep wanting a drink from other people's waterbags.

Water is everywhere around you, but you only see
barriers that keep you from water.

The horse is beneath the rider's thighs, and still
he asks, *Where's my horse?*
                         "Right there, under you!"
Yes, this is a horse, but where's the horse?
                         "Can't you see!"
Yes, I can see, but whoever saw such a horse?

Mad with thirst, he can't drink from the stream
running so close by his face. He's like a pearl
on the deep bottom, wondering, inside his shell,
"Where's the Ocean?"
                         His mental questionings
form the barrier. His physical eyesight
bandages his knowing. Self-consciousness
plugs his ears.
                         Stay bewildered in God,
and only that.
                         Those of you who are scattered,
simplify your worrying lives. There is *one*
righteousness: Water the fruit trees,
and don't water the thorns. Be generous
to what nurtures the Spirit and God's luminous
Reason-Light. Don't honor what causes
dysentery and knotted-up tumors.

Don't feed both sides of yourself equally.
The spirit and the body carry different loads
and require different attentions.
                              Too often
we put saddlebags on Jesus and let the donkey

run loose in the pasture.

Don't make the body do
what the Spirit does best, and don't put a big load
on the Spirit that the body could carry easily.

(*Mathnawi*, V, 1051-1094)

The Churn

The forms and the creatures have a purpose.
God said, *I was a Hidden Treasure,*
and I desired to be known.

Manifestation contains that Desire
to be known. Like a deep truth
inside a lie, like the taste of butter
in buttermilk, that's how Spirit
is held in form.
                      For a long time butter stays
invisibly present in the churn mixture.
Then a Prophet comes with a dasher, or it might be
just someone who has heard the words of a saint
and is connected to that one as an infant is
when it hears its mother. The baby doesn't understand
language, but it knows the voice-sound,
and gradually learns what the talking means.

We're all born dumb. Only God
did not have to be taught to speak,
though Adam learned without a nurse or a mother,
and Jesus came articulate into the world. But most of us
need a lot of attention, much shaking by the Sheikh,
much turning and paddling. Slowly the butter
emerges. Don't throw away buttermilk too soon!
Wait. Keep churning!

Do that work, and you'll begin to hear *inside*
the maundering drunktalk of drunkards
the Presence of the Winemaker, the Host
who served this wine to us.

(*Mathnawi*, IV, 3028-3050)

Letters

Introduction to the Letters

The Letters, or *Maktubat*, is a collection of a hundred and forty-seven letters that, with a few exceptions, are recommendations to governing authorities, or wealthy businessmen, in which Rumi asks favors for his friends and students. The exceptions are letters to family members and letters which counsel young disciples (#24, #54, #62, #144). Letters #54 and #144 are addressed to Rumi's daughter-in-law and son respectively, on the occasion of their marital difficulties. Letter #62 is addressed to two of his sons, Sultan Veled and Allaudin. The first was his eldest son, who eventually succeeded Rumi as the Caliph of the Mevlevis, and who collected and recorded Rumi's works. The second, Allaudin, was implicated in the disappearance or murder of Shams and fell into obscurity. Letter #1 from the Addendum is addressed to Saladin, who was a close friend of Rumi's and whose daughter, Fatima Khatun, married Sultan Veled. Soon after receiving this letter, Saladin died. Rumi led the procession of dancers and musicians to the gravesite, since Saladin had willed that there should be no mourning at his funeral.

In his book, *Veled Nameh*, Sultan Veled has the following poem about Saladin's funeral:

> The Sheikh ordered, "Bring drums
> for my funeral, and tambourines and dancers.
> Carry me into the street with laughter
> and joy, so that everyone will see how
> the people of God go to God and how
> death is cause for song and celebration.
> This death is like lovers whispering."
>
> Everyone obeyed this order, and there was
> no hypocrisy in the delight that day.

The letters are in Persian, with opening titles and salutations usually in Arabic. Two of the letters are entirely in Arabic. In addition, they are ornamented with Arabic quotations from the *Qur'an* and from the sayings of Muhammed, and with spontaneous lines of poetry in Persian and Arabic. The practical and business nature of the letters notwithstanding, the language is highly complex and convoluted. That was the style of the era. It continues to some extent as a convention in present-day Persian, where one can observe an older person addressed as "Your exalted highness," while the speaker refers to himself as "your servant," "this little one," or "your devotee." In our translations we have omitted some of the embellishments, especially when they are repeated within a letter. These translations must, therefore, be considered as excerpts. The title Shah (King), or its Arabic variants was common, and it sometimes became a part of the name of an important, but not necessarily royal, person. Most notable among these are Shah Nematulah of the famous dervish sect, and Sultan Veled.

Another point to mention is that Rumi sometimes refers to older friends as "father" or "brother," and to younger friends as "son," so that Letter #24, for example, may *not* be addressed to Sultan Veled, though it certainly seems to be part of a series that he wrote to the young couple.

According to Furunzanfar, the *Letters* contain the names of thirty-seven well-known authorities and noblemen of the era. Among these is a prince from the clan of Bahram Shah, whom Rumi refers to as "The pride of the House of David." Letters to this individual (#39) often contain elements of Rumi's teachings. Letter #48 is a response to one Haji Amir, who had evidently asked Rumi for a *brief* explanation of the foundations of the Sufi Way.

The very existence of the *Letters* may seem unusual, and some scholars have expressed reservations about the authenticity of many of them, for two reasons. First, we don't have such collections from other well-known Persian poets and, secondly, unlike the communications of other medieval figures, such as Ghazzali and Jahromi, which deal exclusively with matters of religion and philosophy, Rumi's letters are personal and practical. The explanations for both of these concerns may be in the fact that Rumi was not a secular court poet. He belonged to a group of scholars whose primary function was teaching. Legend has it that he did not start reciting poetry until after he had met Shams. Also, he was the founder of a great society and he had many followers, including his eldest son, who carefully preserved the writings, among them these private papers.

There are two extant copies of the *Maktubat* from the time of Rumi, or soon thereafter, one in Konya and the other in Istanbul. A modern edition was published in Istanbul and Teheran in 1937, and a Turkish edition and translation was published by Abdulbaki Golpinali in Istanbul in 1963. A few of the letters are quoted by various authors, including Furunzanfar in his biography of Rumi. There are some partial translations of a few letters by William Chittick (1983), and other brief quotations elsewhere, but this is the first sizable gathering, in English, of these documents.

John Moyne

References

Chittick, W.C. (1983). *The Sufi Path of Love*. Albany: SUNY Press.

Furunzanfar, B.Z. (1981). *Life of Rumi* (in Persian). Teheran: Zavvar Books.

Golpinali, A. (1963). *Letters of Rumi* (in Turkish). Istanbul: Yeni Matbaa.

Nafiz Uzluk, M.F. (1937). *Letters of Rumi* (in Persian, Arabic, and Turkish). Istanbul: Ilmi Publications.

Letter 24

God opens doors.

Dear Son, a delight to all eyes, the pride of both worlds,

May God's Eye watch over you. Accept the salutations and devotion of your father, and know that I am annoyed to hear that you are sleeping outside your house, and that you are not taking proper care of those dependent upon you, those who have been entrusted to you by God, by Allah. It would please me if you would tend to your household. Rain the sweetness of your character so generously on them that some of it spills over onto me.

> Friend! You ease the pain of others,
> but when it comes to us, you are helpless.

One who can deceive a stranger can also deceive himself.

> Even if you can't cure this hurt, be loving,
> or pretend to be. Can't you pretend!

These desires that come quickly and go quickly, this passing unfaithfulness, is not part of your manliness, your strength and compassion. It's not worth the hurt it causes your friends. God willing, this distorted self-conceit will be removed, and you'll see that it is not water you ride your horse toward but a mirage.

Many have made the same mistake. When they get where they think they want to be, they find nothing. They're just far from their wives and children, and dying of thirst, these riders and their horses. Realize this and stop. Even fools learn how to stop. Don't do it! Don't. Don't! That's all.

> A bird looking for a seed
> looks back and forth, left and right,

many times, with its heart so full
of fearfulness that it can't eat.

That horse blanket you're looking at is not equal in value to this
saddle you already own. It's not worth it!

Water has been drawn and poured in a skin
to drink from. Call it your life,
or call it your Friend.

It is to be expected from your virility and your truthfulness that you
will not hurt or abandon those who only wish you well.

I visited Amir Saif ud-Din several times and gave him my assur-
ance that all would turn out. This is not my usual custom. I did it
for you. It may seem to you like a childish game, but I have had
some intuition and vision into the hidden things on this. Every-
thing I've done, I've done only out of my great love for you. I beg
you once more. In the name of Allah, Allah! Don't give any ex-
cuses: Something is "too easy" or "too hard." Someone's level of
intellect is "below" yours. You feel like you're "compromising"
yourself. NO! Care for those who depend on you. You want to
shoot a swift bird in mid-flight, when you can't even take care of
your trained pigeon.

The crime is that I met you, you
who kill the living and visit the dead.

Free your father from writing these letters and worrying about
writing such letters. Let me be free to pray for you instead of this
worrying.

Before the gift is taken away by death,
Accept and give the given which is not just.

Peace be with you, and glory.

Letter 54

God opens doors.

> Your spirit and mine are amalgams melted
> into each other. When you grieve, I grieve.

With God as my Witness, it's true, when my daughter-in-law hurts,
I hurt more. And my gratitude to your father, Saladin, can never
be repaid. The kindness and Light of that Sheikh came from the
Treasury of God.

My one request of you is that when you are annoyed with anyone
about anything, that you not keep it from me. I want to help!

If my dear son, Sultan Veled, does something to hurt you, I'll banish
him from my heart! I won't answer his calling out! I'll forbid him
to come to my funeral! And this is true for anyone else too.

I don't want you to be sad! If anyone says something against you,
remember Allah is on your side. The Ocean cannot be polluted by
a dog's mouth, or a barrel of sugar ruined by one buzzing fly!

If someone doesn't love you openly and praise you, I'll consider
them guilty of slander, and unforgivable! What is due to you and
your father is a hundred times more than anyone can give. I may
smile at such people, but not a true smile, not until they throw their
deceit into the dark water, not until they change and become
humble toward the genuinely holy ones like your father and
yourself. God willing, I'll go to the grave with these public
convictions.

Tell me everything that has happened, every detail, one by one.
You are a temple of Trusting. God comes to us through you and
your children.

Don't any of you be sad, ever!

May Saladin's glory shine
and fill the eyes of lovers,

so that their souls become tender
mixing with the particles of Saladin.

Letter 144

God opens doors.

What I write today is for the consideration of my prince, the light of my eyes and my heart. The whole world is in his trust. Those given into the care of Zachariah are now in his charge. They are his great challenge. I pray that he not take even one misguided action, and that he quickly burn up the grounds of any grievance. I pray that he not for one unintentional, or intentional, breath forget his caring responsibilities, and that if he have a passing unfaithfulness, or some momentary anger in him, let him not speak it, but let it dissolve in his basic goodness, his nobility of spirit, his patience, and his generosity.

A duckling may have only just been born,
but the Ocean touches its chest.

And to save his father's dignity, and his own, let him continue to love his family and to think of every day as the first day of meeting with his love and every night as the wedding night. Let him never think that he has already won the love of his wife and that there is no need for re-winning her. That's the way of shallow people.

It's not difficult to leave the world
and its people,
But I can't leave you!

* * *

I know, intellectually, that you are right
and true,
but a lover's heart is suspicious!

I trust you will keep this letter hidden. Don't show it to anyone.

God knows what is right.

Letter 62

God opens doors.

Dear son, the chosen one, the wise, accomplished, and faithful Sultan Veled. And dear son, Allaudin, the honorable, the noble, the glorious. May your abundance continue. Greetings from your father.

Do not allow any harshness, or rudeness, or controversy, or retribution afterward, to occur between you or toward Sharafuddin, that guardian of culture. Consider your father's views on this, and don't think that I'm fabricating a situation. Remember that Sharafuddin is very dear to me. I have great, *great* confidence in the tolerance and compassion, the generosity and the sense of responsibility of my beloved children. I expect that whatever they say to Sharafuddin will be said in kindness.

For the sake of your father do this: Whenever you are angry, write to me about it and then sleep on it. Do this two or three days in a row when you are angry. Let me hear that you are doing this! I will add this to my prayers for both of you and for all my children, and that my love for you will catch fire and keep growing.

God willing, you will come back here as soon as you can, full of honor and joy and happiness, God willing.

Letter 1 from the Addendum

God opens doors.

God of our loving, God of our intellects, I think often of Saladin, a pivot-point for the two worlds, afflicted now with a disease of the fingernails and toenails. May God heal him.

Graceful cypress, live through this windstorm.
Eye of the planet, be protected
against envious eyes. Soul of the ground
and the sky, be comforted and blessed.

Let your pain go away,
for you are our seeing. Your health
is our health. Your face:
Let that garden freshen.

A pasture, a park on a dry plain.
Let your bodily hurts be absorbed
by our inner lives and become
elegant decorations in there.

Letter 39

God opens doors.

Generosity and goodness and a blessed peacefulness are the right goals for people, but they are *gifts* to the prophets and the saints, gifts worth sacrificing your precious life for.

May these qualities come to you, to live within the royal scope of your intelligence, you the Pride of the House of David. May God prolong your power.

Please accept a thousand greetings and praises from one so devoted and grateful to you that words cannot say the feelings. May God arrange for us to meet again soon.

And let me also say that my friend, the scholar Shamsudin, and his son, Nurudin, since they have met you, cannot contain their excitement, not for a day, not for an hour. They want to be of service to you somehow, but they're shy. One who has met a Beloved King cannot serve other kings. The blade has severed the bone with them, and there's nothing more to be said. They came to me for help, knowing our friendship, and hoping whatever offense in the past they've committed might be forgiven. I hope this is so. I would once again be indebted to you.

Everyone here wants to see you again and serve you, male and female, old and young. We pray that the God who created East and West will make this happen.

God caused us all to be formed from a drop of semen which had no senses, no intellect or eyes, no qualities of leadership or loyalty. That drop felt no grief or joy, no shame and no respectability. God nurtured that senseless speck of sperm in the womb and in subtle ways caused blood to flow in it and packed flesh around it. In that most lonely place with no tool and no hands God carved the head with its delicate ears and mouth and the amazing openings for the eyes. The complicated tongue was put inside. And the cage of the chest was constructed, and in that, the heart, the love-center which is at once a tasty morsel and a whole world, a pearl and an ocean, a slave and a King.

Who can understand how we came from that unfeeling speck to this we are now? God said, "You see how far I have brought you. Don't think that I will abandon you here. I'll take you from this ground and sky to somewhere where the soil is softer and finer than powdered silver and the atmosphere full of lively presences. There, the sky turns and no one gets old. Nothing rots. Nothing dies. And no one needs to sleep. Sleep is refreshment from pain and fatigue, but there is none of that there."

If you can't believe these words, consider the drop of semen. If I were to tell that drop about the world outside of its confinement in the uterus, it wouldn't believe it either! "There are cities with walled gardens. A sun! A moon. There are healthy, powerful people walking about, and blind ones, and sick ones. Think about it, O sperm drop, when you get born out of where you are now, which one of these kinds of human beings will you be?" By no stretch of any imagination could the sperm confidently believe in such a world beyond the darkness of its enclosure. The clot of semen will deny all that I tell it as wishful speculation. It will resist and try to stay where it is, but there is no escape. It must be dragged out of its ignorance. And that's that.

The chief of the Sheikhs sends his salutations. There is never a break in the friendship of those in service. That Union does not depend on their wills. No negligence, no passion or lack of passion, affects it. The Friendship beyond passion is beyond all emotional weather. It's a gift.

> In there they do not feel the sun's heat
> or the sting of winter. No East, no West.

When someone falters, one of these servants will say, "God guide us out of ignorance."

Let the nobility and the breadth of your faith last forever, through the God of both worlds.

Letter 48

God opens doors.

May God's blessing and prosperity continue to be with the Great Master and Man of God, zealous in his faith, Haji Amir. May God make his well-wishing heart a sacred fountain of compassion and inspiration for others. May his friends rejoice and his enemies be eaten up with jealousy. With the Grace of Muhammed, on whom be peace, accept these formalities from your longtime friend, and know that I would love to see your face. May God let that happen *soon*.

> You came late and left early.
> That's the way with wildflowers!

I'm sure, wherever you are, there live within you many pure elements and spirit essences and that those will unite you with blessings and help you search out the high pleasures of God.

> Night is always night and day, day.
> A rosebush, a rosebush. Panther, always panther.

> Someone who becomes a shoemaker
> will be a shoemaker in any city.

You have asked for three lines of commentary on the bases, the conditions, the habits and manners, the *ways* of the Way. No doubt the events and happenings of the material world are fewer and less subtle than the events of the spiritual world. Many thousands of books have been written giving guidelines about outward circumstances, but more need to be written. Some things happen out in the open that are not covered in any of those volumes. If what the body goes through cannot be contained by a thoughtful belt, event so piling on and exfoliating from event, how can I explain in three lines some truth about the *inner* workings?

External events have been written out in three sentences, but none of these sentences has an ending. One sentence is about past states; one about the present; and one about the future. Whichever one you start reading, you can never reach its conclusion. These three sentences inscribe themselves on the tablet of the trivial intellect, while in Universal Intelligence the whole matter is recorded. The inner states are beyond these three sentences on past, present, and future. What mystery can be contained in three sentences!

If God wills, you will be able to experience more than just these two or three states. You'll know the successive, and continuous, inner worlds one after another, revived and refreshed in every moment, delivered from limitation, from predestination, finitude, even from the idea of an ending. All this came to me when you asked for three sentences. Written words cannot contain what I would tell you. Only conversations, and presences. I wish such gnosis could be scribbled in ink on a page! I would certainly write it out and mail it to you! But pens don't dare move toward that discovery. The pages would catch fire!

> Someone in grief can talk about it
> and let the grief go by saying it,
>
> but consider this odd flower
> that has opened for us here.
>
> It can't show its color to us,
> or put its fragrance into the air.

Letter 81

God opens doors.

May the glories of the two worlds stay with you, and the blessings of heaven.

At this time the dervishes have bought a garden, but they are short five hundred dirhems. The owner will not agree to delay the payment for even ten or fifteen days. I considered every possibility for remedying this, but I could not imagine anyone more appropriate than your unique and sacred self!

I feel it is my duty to ask you *first* for this loan, because of your habitual kindness to the dervishes, and to the poor, and your constant looking-forward to that time when the harvest will come in from these goodnesses.

Some people may appear shabby, but they are the kings of the two worlds. You know this. May God protect your intelligence from disenchantment.

Amen, O God of both worlds.

Letter 83

God opens doors.

May the goodness and benevolence of your authority be prolonged.

Sadruddin, the son of one of the nobility, and a keeper of the secrets of God, is well engaged in the study of the sciences. He is progressing with a fine attitude, but he has practical needs that prevent his continuing.

I gave much thought to asking the governing bodies for help with this, and I decided against it, except for this private letter to you.

I come to your stirrup to ask. If you could throw just the shadow of some support across this cause, the spiritual rewards will be infinite, and I will be greatly indebted. May all go well.

Letter 98

God opens doors.

May the life of your lofty assembly and its master, the helper of the oppressed, the friend of the poor, the pride of Khorasan and Iraq, the great teacher, may all your lives be prolonged, and may God give you rewards appropriate to your compassion. I have never forgotten your kindnesses. I am every day more grateful and more drawn to your friendship.

I know you must feel this attraction too, for friendship always comes from both sides, as do all love-motivations. God's Love and the love of people for God are never one-sided. You cannot clap with one hand, or dance with one foot. God loves those, and those love God. It happens simultaneously.

There are many wonders in the hiding place. The nights are pregnant until their results appear in the day-world. There is aching and wanting, and then what is hidden in the invisible world takes shape, and God brings the visible form together with its thinker. If the thought was noble, you will be ennobled. If it was vile, you will be vicious. I know that you know this. It is why you are so compassionate toward those in difficulty. You dress their wounds. You reach out your hand to help them up. May God bless your strength and your service.

You have a servant, Muhammed, who is now in some disfavor with you. He suffers greatly from this separation. Can you forgive him? And offer him a new life back in the community of your servants, and into the Mecca of your presence? He has been a dear son to me, and a faithful brother, and an obedient worker. I ask for your generosity in this.

> To make a free man a slave with your kindness
> is better than freeing a thousand slaves.

May your helping of people in difficulty become infinite.

Letter 116

God opens doors.

> May you stay young and always smiling.
> May the world's heart live happily in yours.

Dear son, stay unshakably happy and excited with life. May God bless you and make you victorious over enemies inner and outer.

You and I owe our support to Husamuddin, yet I have heard that you have been quarreling with him. Husam is like a son to me. For my sake, console him, promise him things. Do this favor for me. Husam grew up with us. He knows his own weaknesses, and his strengths. You may be thinking wrongly of him. Don't be misguided by others. It isn't in his character not to mean well for you.

Don't think of this as an unreasonable request. Even if you think it's a small thing, the slightest argument *can* cause great injury.

The story is told of a warrior whose horse was wounded in battle. The king gave him one of his own horses, an Arabian that the king was particularly fond of. That horse was also wounded. The king showed displeasure.

The warrior dismounted and refused further service to the king. "I did not show displeasure when I risked my life that you might have a victory, but you are irritated that the animal you gave me is hurt! I will serve a King who appreciates my soul. I shall take my jewel to One who knows jewels."

> Your conflict comes from your vanity.
> Be more peaceful, and your life will be at peace.

If I don't hear soon from Husam how pleased he is with you, I shall be mighty hurt!

Letter 79

God opens doors.

May your charity, your benevolence, and your support for the poor and oppressed be abundant, for one who does such good for others will receive double in return. Please accept from this well-wisher such praise and such prayer.

You have been very kind to Sadruddin. May his pure essence and his glory grow. He is very grateful. But now it is hoped that your support will continue. The beginning of giving is wonderful, but it has no end! The new moon is lovely, but the full moon is another thing entirely!

Your eminence knows of my affection for Husamuddin, a trustee of my heart and an extender of time. The love of such people cannot be described by the pen.

It is hoped that, in the same way, Sadruddin may be filled with further gratitude toward you. He will eventually be in a high position, and it will all derive from your kindness! I also remain indebted to you.

May you be a benefactor forever!

Letter 80

God opens doors.

May your constant benevolence and God-fearing goodness be praised and appreciated. Accept my prayers and good wishes.

I am grateful for your sincerity in supporting the poor, especially your support of the dervishes of God, who are thus not distracted from prayer by concerns with money and business. You are like sunlight on them.

At this time, without your knowledge, a number of your relatives have moved into the hut of the dear, devout, ascetic sister. May God perpetuate her chastity!

This has caused great concern among a number of people whom I respect, particularly because of their high regard for you. I ask you to tell your relatives not to stay there at the hut and not to bother the poor sister.

I wanted to bring this request to you in person, but I thought it unnecessary. One such as you is always ready, by nature, to do a good work. In fact, you look for excuses to do so! May you remain a benefactor.

Amen, O God of the two worlds.

Letter 20

God opens doors.

May blessings, goodness, and praise come to the head of the army.

It is said that when Sultan Mahmood's campaign in India was going badly, the Indian troops greatly outnumbering him, that in desperation he fell on his knees praying, "God, if You will give me a victory here, I swear that I will give whatever spoils come from it to the poor."

The One Who Hears granted that prayer. The Indian soldiers, as though a great wind blew through them, felt an unexplained terror, and ran. They left behind weapons and horses and retainers and even the coffers of their treasury. Never had a single battle yielded such a haul of riches.

When King Mahmood told his troops that he had sworn to give all the spoils to the poor, you can imagine the uproar. "Aren't we poor enough? Look at us! We fought hard, and we have nothing! We're an army of poor people!" They made such a strong case that the King hesitated and looked about for counsel.

Suddenly, a wild dervish appeared. Not a poor man begging for food, but one of the God-surrendered poor. The King called him over and told the story of his battlefield vow. The dervish said, "Do what your soldiers want, if you think you'll never want another favor from God, but if you figure you might sometime need more help from God, then do what you said you would do."

I don't know why I'm writing you this story, but it seems good to tell it.

> Before death takes what you're given,
> give away what's there to give.

No dead person grieves for his own death. He, or she, mourns only what he didn't do. "Why did I wait? Why did I not . . .? Why did I neglect to . . .?"

I can't think of better advice to send. I hope you like it.

May you stay in your infinity, and in your successes.

Peace.

Letter 67

God opens doors.

Pride of the nobility and friend of the poor,

God called on someone to mediate His Grace to you. You should be grateful for that. In the same way your mother and father were intermediaries between God and yourself. They nurtured you and helped you develop your graceful body. Just as you are thankful to them, be grateful to a teacher who gives you knowledge-nourishing from God.

It is said that some ascetics once complained to the teacher who was the source of their believing, "We work harder and suffer more than those students of Muhammed. We abstain from our sensual desires more than they do, yet we receive less recognition. Why?"

The great teacher answered, "Devotion and knowing and discipline come as gifts from the life of the Prophets."

"But we honor the prophetic line."

"The Prophets are a single Being. If you deny one of them, you deny all. In the same way that ablutions are for the whole body, if you don't wash one part, you're still dirty. The Prophets recognize and support and blend with each other. There's only One Light coming through the prophetic window. The same Sun shines through the bodies of all those Messengers. If you disbelieve one of them, you're like a bat that says, "Yesterday's sun was fine, but today, I feel shy in the light." The answer to that is that the two suns are identical. The only difference is that you can't be *tested* in yesterday's light.

In the same way, if a snake on the bank says, "I used to swim in the water that formerly flowed in this creek, but I'm not accustomed to this new water," the answer is, "This water and that water are the same, the only difference being that you cannot now be tested as a swimmer in the previous water, which you claim is so different."

May your soul desire to be *in* the sacred water of the Prophets.

Letter 68

God opens doors.

Dear son, Someone-uddin,

May God free you from the grip of demons! Don't you know that, in these days, sitting by yourself in constant seclusion is demonic! Even lions are wary of being long away from friends, and those they trust. This is not a defect in their leonine natures!

I, your father, know something about demons. They don't whisper in my ears. They shout! They tell me things about you, my son, that if I were to see them in a dream, I would never go to sleep. If it were possible, I would come to you. Who told you such practices would help? They won't. Rather, many harmful things can result.

I've warned you before, but you have pushed my advice under the rug. You do not consider the damage that can come through sensuality. This is like the man who argues the pros and cons of Moses's mission and Moses's status in the prophetic line, yet has no compunction about worshipping a golden calf!

I pray for you, and I have one request. Remember that servant of God we both know. Be conscious of the one who died. Otherwise, you will be wounded wherever you go, and deceived by your youth. Your brother was younger than you, but I wish he had told you the truth of his life. Let God reveal what should be seen and destroy what should not exist.

I do not have the nerve to tell anyone what they should do. My mouth is full of words, but I can't say them. My heart is full, but I can't write what is there. Be aware of the ghost of that spiritual King. Don't let the household that was a temple in Mecca become a caravanserai for misguided wanderers. His ghost moans like a lion, conscious of every action of yours, no matter how small. The demons may yet fall on your head! Don't deny anything, and don't misrepresent the facts of your life. Denial is what the demons want. True humanity means breaking this enchantment and holding fast to one's own strength.

If you are embarrassed to come to me, or if I am not available, try to find the great teacher of this time, Husam. Talk to him. Don't let your enemies win!

> When an enemy hears this, he's happy.
> For God's sake, don't make him happy!
> A difficult life is better for someone
> who truly wants to learn. Comfortable
> lives always end in bitterness.

Peace, and God's compassionate blessings, be with you.

Letter 19

God opens doors.

May God prolong His Protection over the king of Princes!

May I bring to your attention the inner nature of prayer? Though ritual prayer is a fine activity, the spirit within the ritual is superior, just as the spirit of a man is infinite, whereas his praying begins and ends. The germ of his praying, though, continues, as God has said of "those who pray constantly."

In this regard, there is the story of those who stopped paying respects to their teacher, because he didn't perform the evening prayer. "If you will not perform it, we will get up and perform it on our own." They did not say this out loud, but a Sheikh knows thoughts without the words being said.

> You may see holy ones down with you on earth,
> but their place is actually higher than the skies.
> Something may appear to be living in the world
> whose spirit resides in the seventh heaven.

Thus, the priest may explain about the ritual prayer: It begins with "praise" and ends with "peace." But the True Sheikh says, *Prayer is union with God, so that no one is there but God.*

The condition for ritual prayer is ablutions with water, but the requirement for understanding the inner spirit of prayer is forty years of denying the wantings, of turning your eyes and your loving into blood, then passing through seven hundred layers of darkness, then being reborn through God's existence into a new life.

> If you cannot sit on the King's throne,
> be a servant holding a tent rope.

If you are not a ruler, be ruled.
If you're not a prophet, be a student of one.

So, if you become inflated with your achievements, if you become
insolent and turn away from the circle of your friends whom you
trust, and if then you think that it's enough to just turn to the altar
and say some prayers, you are like the vision the dervish saw: a
priest and his congregation praying with their backs to the altar.

May God light your head and let you know the reality of prayer,
which is far beyond any form of it.

I am obliged to you for your promise of support for my student,
Nizamuddin. You are kind to watch over him. I wait to hear the
fulfillment. Completion of anything is better than the starting of it.
The intention to praise is good, but the *act* is as the full moon to the
new moon. Bring the new moon to its wholeness!

May God protect you from the robbers of worldly goods and
especially from the robbers of the inner self. There are those who
want to see everyone lost and hopeless like themselves.

> The one with a flaw in his nature
> does not wish others well.

When a new governor goes for advice to a former governor who
has been let go, the latter will counsel in such a way as to cause the
new one to be fired too. There are those who are, like Satan,
deposed governors. In their jealousy and meanspiritedness they
speak oily lies and try to rob our loves of wonder.

> When jealousy reduces someone to salesmanship,
> a person as coarse as canvas is held out
> to us as the beauty of Joseph!

Keep away from such meanness. Trust in God and sow good seeds.
Let them grow and fill your storage bins, as Joseph did. Then,

Before death takes away what's given,
give what's there to give, away.

Among all favors I ask from you, please treat this one as the most important. Planting onions is different from planting saffron. May your good actions grow, the ones you do with complete certainty, the ways you go with true knowledge. God give you grace and compassion.

And God's Peace be with the Prophet Muhammed and his sacred family and with all the Prophets and the Messengers.

Amen, God of the two worlds.

Printed in the United States
by Baker & Taylor Publisher Services